DATE	4/03

THICH NHAT HANH

THE *Joy* of Full Consciousness

Jean-Pierre & Rachel Cartier

TRANSLATED BY
Joseph Rowe

North Atlantic Books
Berkeley California

Published by   www.northatlanticbooks.com
North Atlantic Books   Cover design © Ayelet Maida, A/M Studios
P.O. Box 12327   Text design by Susan Quasha
Berkeley, California 94712   Printed in the United States of America

Originally published by La Table Ronde as *Thich Nhat Hanh: Le Bonheur de la Pleine Conscience*, 2001.
Cover photograph courtesy of Le Village des Pruniers, used by permission of La Table Ronde.

Thich Nhat Hanh: The Joy of Full Consciousness is sponsored by the Society for the Study of Native Arts and Sciences, a nonprofit educational corporation whose goals are to develop an educational and crosscultural perspective linking various scientific, social, and artistic fields; to nurture a holistic view of arts, sciences, humanities, and healing; and to publish and distribute literature on the relationship of mind, body, and nature.

Library of Congress Cataloging-in-Publication Data
Cartier, Jean-Pierre.
    [Thich Nhat Hanh. English]
    Thich Nhat Hanh : the joy of full consciousness / by Jean
 -Pierre & Rachel Cartier ; translated by Joseph Rowe.
        p. cm.
    Includes bibliographical references.
    ISBN 1-55643-420-0 (pbk.)
    1. Spiritual life—Buddhism. 2. Village des pruniers (Buddhist community)   I. Cartier, Rachel. II. Title.
BQ5660.C377 2002
294.3 927 094472—dc21

                                              2002012457

1 2 3 4 5 6 7 8 9 / 06 05 04 03 02

∾ Contents

∾ Foreword

An Encounter with Thich Nhat Hanh
and an Interview with the Authors

It was hard to believe that we were still in the middle of Paris, a ten-minute walk from the nearest Métro station. Only the faintest sounds of traffic could be heard. Birds chirped in the courtyard just outside, and lush spring foliage could be seen through the windows, moving in the breeze. We had become extraordinarily silent, even for a group of meditators. All sounds of stirring and throat-clearing had vanished radically and totally, as if we were under a spell. Less than thirty of us remained for this final part of the weekend meditation retreat, late Sunday afternoon. It was hard for me, an American, to believe in this good fortune of being with Thich Nhat Hanh in such a small group. If such a retreat were taking place in a major American city, there would be hundreds of people.

The spring sunlight suddenly broke through the clouds and poured into the hall, casting shadows from the trees upon the walls. This sitting had been a very long one. I found myself far calmer and more serene than in previous sittings that weekend, even wishing it might last longer.

Thich Nhat Hanh (or "Thay," as he is called by his students) reached slowly to his side with exquisite leisure, picked up a tiny mallet, and struck a single, perfect blow upon the small hand bell he uses to signal the end of a sitting. The sonorous reverberations of this ring seemed to go on forever.

Finally people began to stir. Since this was the end of the retreat, a question and answer session had been scheduled. At first no one seemed to have any questions. His profound stillness and gentle, all-pervading presence in front of us seemed to answer all questions.

Then a woman raised her hand rather abruptly, and launched into a monologue—more commentary than question. About forty, she had that sharply-etched look of many French intellectuals. Her tone had a sad, plaintive quality, with more than a hint of anger. It was clear that she needed to get something off her chest.

"Monsieur, you spoke earlier of the experience of unconditional love for all beings, love for the totality of existence. But try as I might, I simply cannot accept this. It seems like a nice sentiment until you really start to think about some of the terrible things in the world.... I had a good friend who recently died of AIDS. I cannot love that virus that killed him. In fact, I hate it. I hope it is eradicated from existence, and I wish it had never existed. How could I possibly love a thing like that?"

Thay was silent. In this silence, we all felt the weight of this ancient question. And it was as if we basked in his unhurriedness to find an answer. After a long time, he spoke softly:

"You know, we human beings are like a virus. A deadly virus which is destroying this planet. And we—don't *we* need love?"

It was a long time before anyone else asked a question. Finally a handsome, innocent-looking young man with shining eyes, dressed in white, with long blond hair and beard, wanted to know about the prophecy of the coming of Maitreya Buddha—for certain believers, a kind of Buddhist version of the Messiah—and in fact, this young man also wondered if this might not refer to the same event as the return of Christ.

Thay was quiet for awhile, looking around the room, as if searching our faces for signs of the Maitreya.

"It is said that a very great Buddha will manifest in the future. But what does this mean? Do we really know what a Buddha is? Is a Buddha a man? A woman? A god? A historical figure? A mythical figure? And Christ—do we really know what Christ is?

"You see, we have already had so many extraordinary beings, very great teachers who have appeared in this world to help us. And just look at the mess we are still in.

"Surely what we need now is enlightened *community*. We have had many enlightened individuals. But when have we ever seen an entire community which is enlightened? It may even seem impossible.

"But who says this cannot be? How do you know? Why not a family, a village of awakened beings? And then a city, a region—even a whole country. And why not an awakened planet?

"This is the only useful meaning I can find in such prophesies."

This seemed like the time to ask my own question, a question which has been troubling me ever since I became involved with spiritual groups:

"I have frequented several Buddhist sanghas, as well as groups from other spiritual traditions. Much is said and written about surrender or transcendence of ego, and there are many practices relating to this. But nothing is ever said about *collective* ego, and the need to transcend that. What I often see is people surrendering their personal ego to a kind of group-ego, a collective mind-set which seeks to defend and increase itself exactly like an individual ego. But this seems even worse than individual egotism to me, because it so easily leads to conformist ideology, proselytizing, and even fanaticism. How can this be overcome?"

While I was speaking he was looking deeply and directly at me, but as I finished he dropped his eyes. When he began to talk quietly after about a minute of silence, his gaze remained downward, still not looking at me.

"Sangha means community in the Buddhist sense. However, the sangha, like any other kind of community, is no escape from having to deal with ego in all its manifestations. It is a big mistake to think of the sangha as an escape from any problem of being human.

"The traditional practices are intended to help us see through the illusion of ego, whether individual or collective. However—" and here he raised his eyes and looked directly at me—"perhaps we also need new practices."

I was deeply moved, even a bit shaken, because it was as if he had read the thought of my heart. I had said nothing about it to him or anyone in this group, but it happens that one of my main interests is in discovering new practices which have a spiritual dimension, especially those which make use of the voice and body movements in a musical way. Yet virtually everyone in Buddhist (or any other traditional religious) circles I have ever tried to discuss this with seems to consider the very idea either naive or presumptuous. For me, this was like an encouragement to persevere in my search, and not be misled by conservative reactions. Furthermore, as I was to discover later, he himself has introduced a number of new practices into Buddhism. I bowed deeply to him—we bowed deeply to each other—in the ancient *Namaste* gesture, common to Buddhists and Hindus: "I bow to the Divine in you and in us all."

When I met Jean-Pierre and Rachel Cartier, the authors of the present portrait of Thich Nhat Hanh and his community, I mentioned this brief encounter with Thay, and how deeply it had affected me. We were sitting before a large fireplace at their rambling, soulful three-story country home, an ancient converted millhouse in central France, not far from Limoges. With his long, white hair and beard, and calm gravity, Jean-Pierre seems a patriarchal, almost Biblical figure. Rachel's presence complements and enhances this impression, with the warmth, sensuousness, and hospitality of her Jewish-Moroccan desert origins.

Jean-Pierre: The retreat you speak of took place several years ago, right? I doubt if you would be able to converse with Thay in such a small group now. The French-speaking retreats at Plum Village have recently become huge affairs, for he is much better-known in France than he was a few years ago. Of course the English-speaking retreats there have always been large. I gather he is more famous in the U.S. than he is here?

Joseph: That's right. The reasons for this are not clear to me. After all, Buddhism is just as popular in France as in the U.S., and his main community is here. Yet I have the impression even now that most French people, even those interested in Buddhism, seem to have barely or never heard of him. I think it's at least partly because of the tremendous appeal of Tibetan Buddhism in France. It's interesting that his community is in Dordogne, where a major Tibetan monastery is also located. Not only is Dordogne a beautiful region, it is one that has attracted sensitive human beings for at least 17,000 years. Several major Buddhist teachers have been attracted to the same region where those wonderful paleolithic cave paintings are located at Lascaux.

Jean-Pierre: In our first book together, Rachel and I wrote of the large Tibetan monastery in Dordogne, Dagpo Kagyu Ling. We knew Kalu Rinpoche, its founder.

Joseph: Is this how you learned about Thich Nhat Hanh's teaching and community? Did you become Buddhists?

Rachel: No, not at all. Strangely enough, it was when we were staying at a Franciscan monastic community near Assisi. An Italian friend there urged us strongly to go to Plum Village and meet Thich Nhat Hanh. He was right here in France, in the Dordogne area, only a few hours' drive away from our home. We had spent much time visiting and writing about the Tibetan monastery in Dordogne, yet we knew nothing about Thich Nhat Hanh! So it was through St. Francis that we discovered Thay.

Jean-Pierre: So in answer to your question, we are not Buddhists. But we are students of Thay. He has helped us to find the deepest meaning of our own traditions. In my case, Christian; and in Rachel's case, Jewish. Her father was a rabbi.

Rachel: But I also consider myself a Christian. For me,

Yeshua is the greatest rabbi. Just as Mary Magdalene did, I call him *Rabbuni*, "my Rabbi."

Joseph: Certainly the Jewish and Christian traditions are much closer than most people realize, or admit. We often forget that Yeshua himself was a devout Jew, as were most of the early Christians. Yet how do you explain the paradox of a Vietnamese Zen master helping you to discover the deepest truths of Christianity and Judaism?

Jean-Pierre: I'm not sure it can be explained. However, there is one very important fact that stands out: Thay's teaching gives the highest priority to *practice*, not to metaphysics or theology. And it is especially practice which has become so degraded and mediocre in our Western religious traditions. We have all but lost our ancient practices of meditation. And meditation practice is very alive in Thay's tradition.

Joseph: But it is also alive in many other Eastern traditions as well. In fact, you meditated with Tibetan Buddhist and other teachers long before you even heard of Thich Nhat Hanh, and you even wrote books about them. What is it about him and his teaching that seems to have touched you more deeply than the others?

Rachel: The others place a lot of emphasis on ritual and ceremony. We find that somewhat of a barrier.

Jean-Pierre: Yes, neither Rachel nor I find it very helpful to sit through hours of chanting in Tibetan, full of rituals which we don't understand. Of course those are wonderful practices for people who feel called to go deeply into that tradition, and learn its ways. And the teaching is essentially the same. But Thay's practice is much more universal.

Joseph: How does it differ from Japanese Zen practice, which is also much better-known in France? Isn't Japanese Zen just as simple and free of cultural baggage?

Jean-Pierre: Not really, at least not in my experience. Personally, I find Japanese Zen much more austere, and quite Spartan in its demands on the body in sitting practice.

Rachel: Thay says that meditation should be a joy, not another source of suffering.

Jean-Pierre: The practice at Plum Village is also quite rigorous, but it is much more flexible, and gentler with the body—the frequent walking meditation, for example—and it also seems more psychologically skillful, in a way which we find adapted to our own lives. For example, his teaching deals directly with emotions such as anger and fear.

Joseph: Have you ever seen anyone express anger at Plum Village?

Rachel: No, never. At least not that we have seen.

Jean-Pierre: It's hard to even imagine anyone expressing anger there.

Joseph: Does that mean they repress it?

Rachel: No, I don't feel that they repress anger.

Jean-Pierre: Nor do I. But of course that doesn't mean they never *feel* anger.

Joseph: So they don't express it, and they don't repress it. That means there must be a third way to deal with anger. What do you think it is?

Jean-Pierre: Well, people certainly talk about their anger during the weekly sessions, called "Beginning Anew." These community gatherings are almost a kind of psychotherapy.

Joseph: Yes, I appreciate the value of such sharing. But it probably takes place long after the anger has subsided. What I'm wondering is how they deal with anger in the moment it arises. When I am just starting to feel anger rise up in me, how do I practice this third way, which is neither expression nor repression?

Rachel: I once wrote Thay a letter, asking him if there was any way he could help me learn to express anger appropriately. He never wrote back.

Joseph: How do you interpret this silence?

Rachel: I suspect he was saying that he has already answered my question in his teaching.

Joseph: Might this be related to the image of the tree in the storm? [*See the chapter entitled Emotions and Equanimity.*] Its branches wave and whip about wildly in the storm of emotion, yet its trunk and roots are stable, solid, and calm. These agitated branches are like angry thoughts racing about in the mind.

Jean-Pierre: Yes, and the effort we must make is to keep our attention on the trunk and roots, which represent our truest, deepest nature, and not let ourselves be distracted by the branches waving in the storm.

Joseph: So emotions are like weather, sometimes including violent storms? According to Thay, our main task would seem to be to stop confusing this weather with who we are.

Rachel: Yes. But this is easier said than done! My own tendency is to repress anger, which is of course unhealthy. I was asking him if there was a good way to express it. And his answer was silence.

Joseph: Well, it appears that expressing anger does not necessarily reduce it or de-fuse it. I was very impressed by an article I once read about a psychological study conducted with children in a pre-school, where teachers encouraged them to express anger whenever they felt it. They had to call the experiment off, because it was clear that it was making the children far *more* angry, irritable and aggressive. It had exactly the opposite effect than the one they intended.

Jean-Pierre: This seems to be in harmony with Thay's teaching. When we indulge in expression of anger, we are identified with the branches of the tree moving in the storm.

Rachel: And when we repress our anger, we try to ignore the branches and the storm, and cut ourselves off from feeling them.

Joseph: So perhaps we could say that this third way, which is neither expression nor repression, is allowing ourselves to *feel* the raging storm in the mind and body, yet not be drawn into identifying ourselves with these feelings.

Jean-Pierre: And to keep our attention focused on our original nature, which is always present, symbolized by the trunk and roots of the tree.

Rachel: But I feel we have left out one very important thing. Thay also says that in order for this to work, we must develop true love and compassion for ourselves. In our last retreat, he even suggested writing love letters to ourselves when we are angry or frustrated! This sounds odd at first, but it was a tremendous help to me. When I did this practice, I began to see how subtle and hidden my self-aggression is. He gives great importance to being kind to ourselves. This noble goal of non-identification with anger has little chance of working, as long as we continue to secretly harbor a judgmental and aggressive attitude toward ourselves.

Jean-Pierre: One of the things Thay helped me most with was to see how I was still under the influence of hidden habits of guilt and self-judgment. I thought I had left all that behind, along with the catechisms of my very traditional Catholic upbringing—but it was not so. Those early lessons with the priests had made me into more of an expert than I realized: a real master in the practice of subtle guilt. A good example of this was my habit of judging myself for not being more "advanced" on the spiritual path. Of course, it's absolutely necessary to be humble about one's spiritual status. When you find yourself in the midst of an outburst of rage or aggression, it's good to carefully note it—and then, just *return to your true nature of full consciousness*. This is crucial. Thay taught me that you can always return to your true, original nature. Immediately. Just like that. In the space of one conscious breath. No guilt, no self-*judgment*, no regrets about your spiritual shortcomings. Just return. For me, this was radical. I stopped giving any credence whatsovever to messages of guilt, in any form. It made a tremendous change in my life. I used to be very prone to anger, and this has been the case almost all my life. No amount of expressing or venting anger helped, and neither did analysis of its roots in my Catholic guilt. The self-judgment continued. Only this simple spiritual practice stopped it. And since I really stopped it, the anger seems to have vanished along with the guilt.

Joseph: So you think that this whole problem of anger is connected with self-*judgment?*

Jean-Pierre: I'm convinced of it. At least in my own case.

Rachel: It is for me, too.

Joseph: [*pause*] Just thinking about what you've been saying, I realize it's also true for me, and I suspect for most people. It seems to me that there is a lot of feedback between self-judgment and anger, which creates a kind of vicious circle. The seed was planted in early childhood, when I started to believe in the whole self-judgment and guilt paradigm. Then it becomes automatic, so I don't even know I'm doing it anymore. I may even rationalize it, calling it my "conscience." But it creates resentment and rebellion in me. Periodically, this resentment leads to an outburst of rage or aggression, as you pointed out. And then what do I do? I judge myself for this outburst! No matter how subtle the *judgment*, it perpetuates the resentment, and the vicious circle continues. Techniques such as psychoanalysis usually fail to break it, because they merely transfer the self-*judgment* to "progress" or "cure" in that domain.

Jean-Pierre: What *can* break this circle is returning to your breath, returning to full consciousness, here and now. Total acceptance of the present moment. It's always available.

Rachel: And being kind to yourself. It may sound redundant, but it's so important.

Joseph: Some people may confuse this kindness with some kind of softness, or self-indulgence.

Rachel: No, this love for oneself has absolutely nothing to do with self-indulgence or sentimentality. Anyone who has met Thay, or knows anything about his life, knows that he hasn't an ounce of sentimentality in him. His tenderness is that of an immensely strong person, not a soft one. The practice of kindness to oneself is actually very demanding. Many people at Plum Village have told us how difficult it was for them at first.

Joseph: This brings us to the subject of the community around Thich Nhat Hanh. My own encounter with him suggested that he considers community to be of crucial importance for human evolution. I visited Plum Village after this encounter, and found it to be a beautiful and powerful experience, just as you did. But it seems to me that it's still a very traditional Buddhist monastery. Vows of celibacy are taken, and men and women live separately. What relevance does this have for the future evolution of humanity?

Jean-Pierre: I do believe that Thay's vision of community is relevant to human evolution, but we have to be careful not to look for it in the wrong places. I don't feel that it is to be found so much in the outer forms of community structure. It's much deeper than that. It's true that Thay's community is extremely traditional in certain ways—for example, the monastic rules of celibacy, etc. But this is simply his culture, the religious tradition of his people. It has little or nothing to do with the real gift he has to offer.

Joseph: Do you think he adheres to the ancient Buddhist doctrine (also common in Christianity and Hinduism) which considers those who live the monastic life as a kind of spiritual elite?

Jean-Pierre: Absolutely not. The role of monks and nuns at Plum Village, in relation to the lay community, is only to help them strengthen their spiritual practice, not to guide them from some supposedly superior spiritual position. Which brings us back to practice, the essence of Thich Nhat Hanh's teaching. His genius, I think, is to infuse the old practices with a fresh, new spirit. And to invent new practices.

Joseph: Yes, and these are detailed in your book. I guess my real question is: what is the way to the "enlightened community" that he talks about? And how does this manifest in his own community at Plum Village? You seem to be saying that it is in the practices, not in the organizational structures.

Jean-Pierre: Yes. But we must not neglect to mention the lay communities, which are now quite numerous in many countries. We participate in one of these, which has recently begun in our area. They are often informal and small, but some of them have become very organized, and hold retreats of their own.

Rachel: And the people in them are not necessarily Buddhists at all. There are Christians, Jews, Moslems, even atheists, as well as Buddhists.

Joseph: Looking at the magazine you showed me from Plum Village, I saw an article about a community in Israel founded by Thich Nhat Hanh. They held a retreat where Jews and Palestinians meditated together.

Rachel: Yes. You know, one of the most beautiful things about Thay's approach to community is that he is not trying to propagate Buddhism. On the contrary, he tells his Western students to first investigate the real, often lost, teachings of their own tradition. Jean-Pierre and I have been deeply affected by this. He says, "Delve deeply into your own spiritual heritage.

You will find hidden treasures there." And he gives us the practices which help us to find and recognize these treasures.

Joseph Rowe
Paris-Parnac
JUNE, 2002

1 ∾ *The Taking of Vows*

*T*here are twelve of them, nine young women and three young men. They stand, forming three rows in the center of the vast *zendo*, or meditation hall. Colorful paper ribbons have been hung around the hall for the occasion. Around them are gathered members of their families, as well as the 112 monastic members of the Plum Village community—monks on one side, nuns on the other. They stand with impressive solemnity and repose, their shaved heads gleaming under the electric lights.

The twelve young postulants still have all their hair. They are dressed in their finest, especially the women, who wear long, beautiful gowns, as if attending a wedding.

The gong sounds three times, and everyone begins a solemn chant. Curiously, this Buddhist chant uses the melody of the *Veni Creator,* a medieval plainchant which used to be sung in Latin on Pentecost.

It is the beginning of the ordination ceremony at Plum Village (Village des Pruniers) in the region of Dordogne in southern France, on this morning of May 5, 2000. The chanting continues for some time, one chant after another, reciting excerpts from the great Buddhist sutras.

Then Thich Nhat Hanh, Zen master and spiritual teacher of the community, comes forward. He wears the same simple brown robe as the other monks and nuns. Today it is adorned with orange, marking the ceremonial occasion.

Immediately, one is struck by his extraordinary presence. As he walks slowly toward the group of young monastic aspirants, one feels that his every movement is a form of meditation.

He begins to address the community of lay persons, monks, and nuns, who have gathered together here from the three hamlets which comprise Plum Village. He poses ritual questions, which have ritual forms of response:

> "Is the entire community present?"
> "Yes, the entire community is present."
> "Is the community in harmony?"
> "Yes, the community is in harmony."
> "What is the reason for this gathering of the
>   community today?"
> "To perform the ordination of the postulants."

A nun reads the names of these twelve candidates. Then *Thay*, as he is called by his students (a Vietnamese word which means "teacher"), asks if there is unanimous agreement to welcome these aspirants into the monastic community. Silence means agreement. If anyone has an objection, this is their last chance to voice it. A deep silence reigns for a moment over the assembly.

Then, one after another, the twelve postulants come before Thich Nhat Hanh and do four prostrations, "as a sign of gratitude toward all beings, living and inanimate."

Another assistant comes forward, carrying a chalice of water which holds a rose. Thay places his hands upon each postulant's head, and then uses the rose to sprinkle a little of the water on their foreheads. He asks questions in a low voice, to which they reply. Then he cuts a small lock of hair, accompanied by gongs, and the singing of hymns. The candidates then perform three more prostrations before receiving their robes. They place their robes on top of their heads, where they will remain for the rest of the ceremony. These simple, humble garments will constitute their essential wardrobes for the rest of their lives.

Now comes the most solemn moment of all, the taking of vows. An assistant reads the precepts of the Buddha and asks the postulants if they vow to follow them the rest of their lives. In unison, they answer:

"I do."

This means they must refrain from killing, stealing, and eating meat. They must be celibate and renounce worldly distractions, luxury, the wearing of jewelry, and the lure of consumerism.

The ceremony is over. Festive drums now join the gongs, along with hymns of joy and gratitude.

The ceremony of shaving the head will take place later in the day, in privacy. Some of the women have beautiful long hair down to their shoulders. While eating lunch with them a little later, we are struck by the odd fact that we now seem to have trouble recognizing them individually. Their hair has not yet been cut, but it is as if they have already taken refuge in that moment only hours away—the event which traditionally marks the passage from the worldly life to that of the renunciate.

It is a little later in the afternoon. A small wooden footbridge stretches across the pond, where lotuses are just beginning to bloom. On a ledge next to the bridge, someone has placed a rather surprising object: a baby doll, of the type little girls often play with. It represents the newborn Buddha—for today is also the birthday of Gautama Shakyamuni, known as the Buddha. Two large basins full of rose petals have been placed in the middle of the footbridge. Those who wish to honor the Buddha-baby walk to these basins, fill a long wooden dipper with the rose petals, and sprinkle them over the head of the doll. There are many people waiting their turn to perform this ceremony, and it takes up a large part of the afternoon.

Thay is the first to go to the bridge. He walks slowly, two children holding his hand on each side. His face, which had been so solemn during the earlier ceremony, is now beaming with a huge smile—one of those smiles which actually startle you, because they spring from such depths of the heart. As we are to discover, children are one of his greatest sources of happiness. He loves to play with them and look deeply into their eyes. This explains why a major part of his life has been devoted to helping Vietnamese orphans, feeding and caring for them, and healing their memories of the misery they have experienced.

As Rachel and I watch him now, we are both struck by the same thought: this man, so serious and noble in other contexts, this activist for peace, this brilliant poet, Buddhist scholar, author of many books, who is revered as a teacher by disciples around the world—this man has remained a child at heart. We cannot help being reminded of the words of Jesus: "Unless you become as little children, you shall not enter into the Kingdom of Heaven."

2 ∾ A Buddhism of Social Action

*W*ho is he? This will prove to be a difficult question to answer. He does not like to spend time discussing his life story, nor does he give interviews for publication. He has kept a journal all his life, but only allowed a small portion of it to be published: the years from 1962 to 1966, under the title *Fragrant Palm Leaves* (Parallax Press; Riverhead Books). The title alludes to the ancient use of palm leaves to record sutras, such as those of the Buddha.

These journals have been a great discovery for us, and we feel fortunate that he allowed them to be published. They communicate a vivid sense of his life as a young monk, and also of his experiences as a peace activist. He relates how he had to struggle with the incomprehension of his own monastic hierarchy, as well as with the forces which were promoting and maintaining the horror of the Vietnam war.

Born in 1926, he was only sixteen when he became a monk. Yet even at this age, his passion for truth and justice began to create difficulties with some of the more conservative Buddhist authorities. Having a deeply compassionate and mystical nature, he has always believed that Buddhism is not merely a path of individual salvation. For him, the compassion taught by the Buddha also implies social action. This means that

Buddhism must go deep within itself to find the authentic sources of such action—but it does have the resources to help with the great social problems which cause so much human agitation and misery. Of course we must find peace within ourselves. But this inner peace is not just for our own welfare or salvation—if it is authentic, it will also help us make peace a reality in our outer world. Only in this way can we oppose violence without becoming violent ourselves. Every truly religious human being has a duty to struggle against injustice, poverty, ignorance, and war. Thay is well-versed in the latter, for he was deeply involved in the effort to end the long, terrible war which tore his country apart.

In 1956, when he was only thirty, he was able to sidestep the antagonism of orthodox Buddhists by founding a new monastery. Its name was Phuong Boi, which means "Fragrant Palm Leaves." Even today, his nostalgia for it is deeply touching—hearing him speak of it, one has the feeling of a paradise lost. Working with a group of very close and devoted companions, he labored to clear a space in the jungle for the monastery to be built. They had decided to establish it as far from civilization as possible, and make their living by cultivating tea. They chose the central region of Vietnam, in the lands of the mountain tribes. In those days it was still a remote and unspoiled region, and they sometimes saw tigers.

But alas, the life of this little paradise was to be a short one, for the war came and found them. This island of peace seemed to annoy both sides, communist rebels and government troops alike. Barely had the tea plantation begun to operate, when they were forced to leave and seek refuge in Saigon. Afterward, the fighting destroyed most of what they had built, and the jungle reclaimed the rest.

Some years later while he was in the United States, Thich Nhat Hanh still experienced great emotion when he thought of this loss:

> *Suddenly I thought of Phuong Boi, and my heart was filled with nostalgia. But enough, enough! Phuong Boi has slipped through our fingers. Though we grieve for every thicket, for every meadow, for every path, we have never truly lost Phuong Boi. It will always be inscribed in our hearts as a sacred reality. Wherever we go, the simple utterance of the words,* Phuong Boi, *moves us to tears.*

Leaving it was one of the most painful decisions he had ever had to make. He had so much wanted to help his war-threatened country by establishing an oasis of peace. Now he was constantly faced with the growing terror and misery of his people: villagers killed by bombs and napalm, and the countless other atrocities committed by both sides. As he witnessed the suffering and death of children, his resolve and longing for peace only became stronger. Neither side in the conflict wanted anything to do with him. The communists rejected him because he was a Buddhist, and the American authorities did not take kindly to his incessant appeals for an end to the fighting.

He left Vietnam in 1961, travelling to the U.S. to bring his message of peace. At the universities of Columbia and Princeton, he taught Vietnamese language and culture, as well as Buddhist psychology. This ended in 1963, when his friends implored him to return to Vietnam and help in the struggle for peace, which had become urgent. In those days the war was still in its early stages, before the massive escalation by the U.S. government in 1965.

From that time on, he found himself on all fronts. He knew that the countryside was being subjected to great suffering— it was not rare for nationalist forces to occupy and terrorize a village by day, and communist forces by night. He deeply understood the bewilderment and misery of the hapless peasants, who only asked to be left in peace to cultivate their rice and vegetables. He saw their houses destroyed by bombs and their harvests ruined or confiscated by soldiers, in a climate of growing harshness and cruelty.

Yet this did not discourage him, and he lost no time in lamenting the situation. Making use of his exceptional talent as an organizer, he founded the School of Youth for Social Service in Saigon in 1964, and began to send monks, nuns, and lay volunteers into some of the most vulnerable and destitute villages. These young people worked hard to establish schools and clinics there, winning the villagers' hearts by sharing their humble lives. For Thay, this was authentic, engaged Buddhism. He believed that if the Buddha himself were to encounter a situation such as that in Vietnam, he would not simply withdraw and meditate in a temple. The temples housed his statues, but his dynamic, living presence was to be found among those whose compassion impelled them to help the villagers, working to save what could be saved, and rebuild what had been destroyed. As he wrote in his journal:

> To isolate oneself in a temple is useless for those who wish to know the Buddha. Those who withdraw like this only demonstrate that they are not true disciples of the Buddha. The Buddha is to be found where there are beings who suffer.

This School of Youth for Social Service was created in collaboration with teachers and students, both secular and religious. It was a great success, and by the end of the war counted over 10,000 volunteers working in many villages. But sadly, the communists felt threatened by this organization. They abolished it, just as they did the Boi Press, a publishing house which counted Thich Nhat Hanh as one of its authors, as well as its founder and inspiring guide.

His engagement took place on other fronts as well—when floods devastated a valley, he hastened to the area, accompanied by many volunteers, all working with mud up to their knees, in an effort to help the peasants salvage what they could.

When the "boat people" began to flee Vietnam, only to be rejected everywhere they went, and attacked by pirates at sea, he organized missions to go to their rescue. He succeeded in outfitting three ships, which searched for endangered refugee boats, and patrolled alongside them. Accompanied on these voyages by Sister Chan Khong, he welcomed the emigrants aboard his ships and helped them to search for a country of asylum. In this quest, he had to deal with the callousness of national maritime police forces. On previous occasions, when refugees had arrived on foreign shores in desperate condition, thinking they were saved at last, these authorities had forced them back into the sea, where they drowned. Thich Nhat Hanh himself experienced being expelled from Singapore with hundreds of refugees on the three ships, with no idea where they would go next. "We were hunted and chased like animals," he wrote later. In spite of these overwhelming obstacles, his strong determination and credibility had the effect of arousing international indignation at the plight of these desperate people, resulting in thousands of lives being saved.

When the war was over, he was forced into exile by the new regime. Nevertheless, continuing to work without any fanfare, he found the means to raise money to save starving Vietnamese children and orphans, as well as artists who had been languishing in prisons. In his book *For a Future to Be Possible*, he writes:

> *The war created thousands of orphans. Instead of raising money to build orphanages, we decided to approach people in the West to sponsor children. We had already found village families who were willing to take care of an orphan, if we could provide six dollars a month for the child's food and schooling. Whenever possible, we tried to place a child in the home of a relative, perhaps an aunt, uncle, or grandparent. The six dollars enabled them to have enough to eat and attend school, with some left over to help other children there. These orphans had the great advantage of growing up in a family environment, for life in an orphanage was almost like that in an army camp. This is an example of how we can improve things by searching for new ways to practice generosity.*

For Thich Nhat Hanh, compassion includes the perpetrators as well as victims of suffering. In one of his trips to America, he met with veterans of the Vietnam war. This resulted in his leading special meditation retreats for war veterans—with such success that they continued and grew for many years. Some of these men were tormented by the atrocities they had witnessed, others by those they had committed themselves. Thay recalls many stories, such as that of the junior officer who had not been able to get over the horror of seeing more than 400 men of his battalion killed in a single day. Another man confessed how, after losing a bloody battle, he and his men took revenge on the people of a certain village by leaving booby-trapped cakes there. It was children who found them, and were blown to bits. He was still overwhelmed by the anguish and guilt of his role in this. Other veterans had seemingly lost all ability to speak of their suffering; and still others had developed physical symptoms, such as anorexia.

These ex-soldiers, tormented by what war had forced upon them, found in Thay's fellowship a peace they had not felt for many years. With him, they began to understand that even executioners and torturers are the victims of an inhuman system, and of a causal chain of circumstances. In his presence, they at last felt understanding and forgiveness. This happened largely in silence, through the simple routine of life at the meditation retreat: learning to be aware, to feel the earth beneath one's feet, to eat in silence, to see flowers and the deep blue of the sky as if for the first time, and to smile again.

> *Every side is our side. There is no evil side. These veterans, with their war experiences, are the burning flame of a candle whose light reveals the roots of war, and the way to peace.*

The Buddhism of Thich Nhat Hanh cannot be understood in isolation from social action. In his view, the Buddhist principle of right action necessarily has a social dimension. Yet such action must arise from the depths—depths which are awakened through the practice of sitting meditation, walking meditation, and full consciousness in the midst of action.

3 ∾ *In a Single Leaf*

It is six o'clock. In the chilly half-light of this spring morning, shadows are moving with a curious languor. Robed men and women, arriving from their separate monasteries, are walking with exquisitely slow paces towards the meditation hall.

This is the first morning of the annual retreat for French-speakers, which coincides with the week of Easter. It seems like an ascetic situation at first, until we get more used to it. Granted, you do have to get up at five-thirty A.M.—and even this is a concession to non-monastic visitors like ourselves, for the monks and nuns normally arise at five o'clock.

The day begins with a sitting meditation in the great zendo. This is always followed by a period of walking meditation. "One step, breathe in. One step, breathe out." We walk with extreme slowness around the entire perimeter of the zendo, until we come back to our places. And the day unfolds in this tempo, filled with awareness and silence. It is punctuated by the chanting of sutras, meals eaten silently, teachings by Thay, and a final sitting and walking meditation around five o'clock that afternoon.

What makes the greatest impression on outsiders who come to these retreats—and we have heard many testimonies to this effect—is the atmosphere of profound peace, of loving kindness, and of relaxed concentration which permeates every aspect of life in the hamlets (described more fully in Chapter 5). At first we feel something almost like annoyance, because it is such a radical break from the deep-seated habits of tension and hyperactivity with which we live, often without being aware of them. Here, life flows like a vast and tranquil river. It is as if we have undergone a radical change of climate. And the nature of this change becomes clearer as the retreat goes on.

It seems that this new climate enables the teachings to penetrate to our very depths. Our basic task is simply to open to this new way of life, and then allow an understanding to unfold naturally within us. It is an understanding which becomes more and more alive as the retreat goes on. The specific content of one's meditation is of secondary importance—it could be inspired by a piece of wood, a shell, a tree, a river, or the look of a child....

For Buddhists, probably the best-known example of such content is the "meditation on a pippala leaf." This refers to the pippala tree under which Gautama Shakyamuni was sitting when he awakened, and thereafter became known as the *Buddha* (Sanskrit, the "awakened one"). On our retreat at Plum Village, we decide to begin with this meditation for several reasons: because several people here have told us how it inspired their practice of Buddhism; because it is a tradition which is attributed to the Buddha himself; and especially because of Thay's lucid commentary on it, both in his spoken teachings and in his book *Siddhartha*:

> He smiled and raised his eyes to see a pippala leaf outlined against the blue background of the sky, fluttering in the breeze, as if signaling to him. Looking intensely at this leaf, he saw in it the presence of the sun. Indeed, without sunlight and warmth, this

leaf could not exist. This exists because of that, and that exists because of this. At the same time, he saw the presence of the clouds in this leaf. Without clouds, no rain; and without rain, no tree. With this same intensity, he saw the Earth in this leaf, and saw that it also contained space, time, and mind. Its very existence was a wonder and a miracle...

Though it is our habit to think that leaves are born in the spring, Gautama realized that this leaf had always existed, implicit in the sunlight, in the clouds, and in the tree itself. Hence this leaf had never really been born at all. Seeing this, he saw that his being, too, had no origin. Like the leaf, he simply manifested through a temporary form, which had its origin in time. Yet neither he nor the leaf had ever been born, and hence they could never die. In this realization, all concepts of birth, death, appearance, and disappearance dissolved. His own true nature, as well as that of the leaf, revealed itself directly. Then he saw how the existence of one phenomenon makes all other phenomena possible, through interdependence. One single manifestation contains all others. In truth, they are all one...

This leaf and his body were one, since neither possessed a separate self, existing independently of the rest of the universe. Perceiving the interdependent nature of all phenomena, Siddhartha also realized their essential emptiness: nothing that exists is endowed with any sort of self separate from other things. And he understood that the key to freedom is in these two principles: interdependence, and no-self.

Can we really add anything to this? The millions of words that have been written on Buddhism, the teachings of countless thousands of masters over two and a half millennia, together with all the learned commentaries and interpretations, are ultimately no more than variations on this theme. These variations have multiplied exponentially through the ages, comprising thousands of tomes and embracing all subjects.

Yet this complexity only brings us back to the simple truth that everything is contained in a single leaf: the sun, the clouds, the Earth, the Buddhist commentaries, all of time and space. As Thay says, when you touch a flower, you touch the sun, without burning your fingers.

Yet it is also true that the compost is present in that same flower. This form could not have been produced without dirt, decay, and death. And the flower contains the compost in another sense, for someday it will become compost again. Furthermore, that compost also contains the flower, for it once was flower, and can become flower again. Once we can see the principle of interdependence at work here, then we can see it in ourselves.

In his teaching this morning in the zendo at the New Hamlet, Thay develops this theme of flower and compost:

> *There are positive states of mind, such as love and understanding. And there are negative ones, such as fear, despair, and jealousy. We contain both flower and compost within us. If we are skilled in the art of organic gardening, then we need not abhor filth or refuse.*
>
> *The fear, anger, and suffering in us are like useful compost. We must not try to throw them out the window. They are quite necessary in order for flowers like compassion, joy, and happiness to bloom in us. This*

is the non-dual view which we must embrace. It is the basis of all our practice. Without it, we will continue to suffer. We will continue to believe that we have to get rid of these negative states in order to be happy. On the contrary, it is very important to accept them. The essential art which we must learn is that of transformation. With skill, it is entirely possible to transform negative things into positive ones. And we must not forget that positive things also become negative ones: flowers will someday become compost again.

With experience in meditation, it is possible to see the rotting compost already present in the flower. But those who have not learned to meditate may need ten days or so to learn to see the flower as compost, and the compost as flower. Experienced meditators have the advantage of not having to wait, for they can see this more quickly.

What I am proposing to you now is extremely important. It is something I practice myself: Whenever something occurs in your body or in your mind that might cause you suffering, do not be in a hurry to get rid of it. first, awaken the energy of full consciousness in yourself. This will enable you to recognize, to accept, and even to smile at this visitor, and say to it, "My dear, I know you're there. I'll take good care of you, I know what to do." This is a marvelous practice. We must take good care of our negative states of mind, as well as our negative states of body.

So we see that suffering has its role to play, just as death has its role to play, in making life possible. We *should train ourselves to see things in this way all day, every day. When we look at a cloud, a flower, or a loved one, we should look deeply, so as to be in touch with this non-dual nature which is the basis of everything.*

From now on, you have the eye of the Buddha with you. You can use it. It is always available to you. The Buddha has been transmitted to you, and is also already within you. Your legs have become Buddha-legs. This means that you now have the power to walk upon the Earth with happiness, gentleness, and kindness. And when you walk like this, you walk with the legs of the Buddha. This is something which is entirely possible for you now—you can learn to walk like this.

When Thay finishes speaking these words, a vast silence fills the hall. In it, we feel a new faith and confidence arising. The words he is always repeating are finally sinking in: "This is possible now." Happiness is possible, not in a few months, not in a year, or ten years, but right here and now. This is not an abstract idea to be considered and reconsidered. It is a practice. *Practice* is a word which recurs often at Plum Village. Here, practice is an everyday reality which is constant, simple, and available to everyone, though they may have abandoned or forgotten it for a time.

Mystics of all traditions are agreed on this point: that the highest ideal and goal of a spiritual life must be to live in the Present, at all times and in all places. Unfortunately, this profound teaching is often misunderstood, producing feelings of guilt or discouragement for one's failure to live in the present. When we see how easily our mind becomes distracted, racing off in all directions, we may despair and lose faith in our spiritual potential.

Thich Nhat Hanh's teaching can free us of this self-judgment. Although it is certainly true that our mind has a powerful tendency to wander, it is just as true that at any instant, we have the possibility of simply returning to *full consciousness*. This return is free of all guilt or regret for our distraction. It is utterly simple, and Thay offers simple and practical means for helping us to make it a reality in our lives.

But first let us return to the flower. It has still more to teach us about the nature of emptiness, which is related to the subject of living in full consciousness.

All the great Buddhist teachers have spoken of emptiness. According to the monk Narashina, who lived in the second century c.e., "Emptiness is what makes everything possible." The celestial boddhisattva Avalokita (Avalokiteshvara) is supposed to have said: "All things are empty." To which Thich Nhat Hanh answers: "Yes, Lord Avalokita—but empty of what?" Thay's teaching about emptiness, or *shunyata*, is that it necessarily implies being empty *of something*.[1]

> *A glass may be empty of tea, and yet be full of air, or full of space. Hence to be empty is to be empty of something.*

So our flower is full, and yet it is also empty of something: a separate existence. It cannot exist apart from the totality of existence. The only being it possesses is an inter-being with all that is. Hence the flower is full of the universe, yet empty of any sort of separate selfhood.

The Buddha placed great emphasis upon emptiness, yet he also warned his disciples against becoming trapped by this notion, making it into an absolute. It should be regarded as a valuable and helpful understanding, yet never made into an object of veneration. Emptiness is especially precious in offering us insight into the nature of birth and death, a question which often obsesses us.

We return again to the flower: it would be wrong to say that it was born of emptiness, for nothing can arise from nothingness. The flower is the outcome of a series of manifestations which go back as far as time itself. But we would also be mistaken to accept the conventional conclusion that it was born on the day its bud appeared, or began to open. This flower has always been. It was in the seed which itself came from a previous flowering. It is also in the wind which carried that seed to the right soil, in the rain which fell from the sky to water it, in earth, and in the sky itself. That which we call "flower" is simply a form which manifests when all the right conditions are present.

On walls at Plum Village, we often see this reminder: "You are not a creation, you are a manifestation." What applies to the flower also applies to human beings. We are "born" when all the right conditions come together to produce this birth. And these conditions include death, which is necessary in order for this new human manifestation to occur.

We will have more to say later on this theme of birth and death, but if we understand this simple reminder, we can already feel a radical change taking place in our view of ourselves and of the entire universe.

As soon as I stop believing in myself as a separate "me," and see that I am one with the totality of being, I begin to see the world around me with different eyes. That insect walking on my desk right now ... I am not separate from it. I can no longer just crush it under my thumb, as if it were a trifling object outside of me. I am also one with the wind, the plants, the stones, and the ocean. I can no longer content myself with thinking "I exist," for in truth, as Thay says, I *inter-exist*. No longer can I regard myself as separate from the other men and women around me. And this discovery of *inter-being*, when grounded in practice, can only lead me to a deeper understanding of what love really is.

"Understanding," Thay says, "leads to compassion and love. And these lead in their turn to right action. In order to love, we must first have understanding."

4 ∾ Choosing the Monastic Life

*I*t is now 7:30 A.M., marking the end of the meditation session. Already on this first morning of the retreat, one can see the effect on the faces of the others. Their relaxed and calmly radiant expressions show the benefits of this time of silence, devotion, and kindness. In the days to come, we will all be partaking deeply of the everyday atmosphere of the monks and nuns of the three hamlets.

Most of the monastics are fairly young. Many are Vietnamese, but there are also a number of Dutch, Germans, Canadians, and French—the latter more recent arrivals for the most part. Curiously, French monastics are a minority here, in spite of the great interest in Buddhism in France, especially of the Tibetan variety.

This is not an easy life they have chosen. Not that Buddhism values the practice of austerities as a spiritual path in itself. The Buddha himself warned against this in his famous discourse at Benares:

> O monks, there are two extremes to be avoided by anyone who would live a spiritual life. What are these two extremes? One is a life ruled by pleasures, devoted to lust and gratification—this is base, degrading, vain,

ignoble, and profitless. The other is a life of self-mortification—this is saddening, unworthy, and profitless. By avoiding these two extremes, O monks, the Tathagata² has gained knowledge of the Middle Way which offers insight and wisdom. It is the way which leads to peace, to knowledge, and to the supreme enlightenment of Nirvana.³

The importance of discrimination between pleasure and happiness in the Middle Way is explained by Thich Nhat Hanh in his commentary on the *Sutra on Knowing the Better Way to Catch a Snake:*

We must make a distinction between indulgence in pleasure, and the serenity of joy and happiness. Excessive indulgence in pleasure can be harmful, whereas joy and happiness, on the contrary, are the very foundation of our physical and spiritual well-being,—and a guide on our path of practice.

The monks and nuns of Plum Village have renounced the pleasures of modern consumerism, yet they also avoid the kind of austerities sometimes practiced in Christian and Hindu monastic traditions. However much they may experience joy and happiness, there is no doubt that new visitors to Plum Village see daily life there as quite austere in comparison to their own comfortable lifestyles.

The shaven heads are the most visible symbol of self-renunciation. A deeper one is the meagerness of their possessions: a few personal objects, and the habits they wear. Monastics sleep in rooms shared with others, eat strict vegetarian meals in silence, and spend hours a day in what is called "work meditation," also performed in silence as much as possible. They have few recreations, few pleasures, no television, stereo, or other entertainment, and of course no sexual life.

This is a life which most of us would regard as severe in its renunciation—yet the relaxed expressions and ready smiles of these renunciates is striking in comparison to the faces one meets in the outside world.

Interested in knowing more about these people, we obtained permission to interview a number of them. We began with three young Vietnamese women, who spoke to us on condition of total anonymity. Therefore we shall refer to them as Sister X, Sister Y, and Sister Z.

All three expressed very similar motives for coming here—we saw themes in their stories which were to recur strikingly in those of other, quite different nuns and monks we met later. The primary theme, common to all of them, was a profound dissatisfaction with what life in a consumer society has to offer.

We begin with Sister X, a young woman with a reflective expression, wearing a woolen cap to protect her head from the cold:

> *When I compared my family with others, I saw that most of us made a good living. My parents were doctors, and had many possessions. We lived a prosperous consumer lifestyle common in Canada. But when I looked at my parents' lives, I got a feeling of unreality. It was strange: they would get up in the morning, go to work, shop at the supermarket, come home, watch television, and go to bed ... and then get up the next day and do the same things. They aged slowly. Their lives were always the same. I wondered how they could continue on like this.*

All around me, I saw people who seemed to never reflect or wonder about life. They simply said: "Our parents gave birth to us, and here we are." This gave me no satisfaction, for I had a need to understand.

Sister Y:

I was born in the U.S., where I had a comfortable life. But I saw little happiness in those around me. As far as my family was considered, my path in life was already laid-out: I would simply do well in my studies, get a good job, and start a family ... in other words, continue in their own pattern, having children who would do the same. But I wanted to know what lay beyond this structure which was closing me in.

And Sister Z:

I come from an acquisitive family. My parents were constantly accumulating possessions, and I had the feeling that something was not right. Our space was always cluttered with them, and there were many things we never even used. We moved many times, and it was always an agonizing process. We had to pack everything, and were so afraid of forgetting something. And we were always buying more and more.

Naturally there were some good things among all these possessions, but most of them were really useless. And we had to protect them. Whenever someone left my father's house, they had to activate the security system. Here at Plum Village I never use a key, yet I feel far more secure. I was always afraid there, but here I don't hesitate to walk out, even at night, without the slightest fear.

Our attic and cellar were full of stuff, piled up with papers and books. It always depressed me to go in there. I needed space. And freedom.

Now I see the consumer lifestyle as a kind of prison, a prison in which my family has become trapped, like so many others. When so much of your life revolves around television, it's difficult not to be a consumer. I wanted to escape from this pattern, but I didn't know how.

These three young women all come from upper middle-class Vietnamese families in North America. They had all been struck by the same observation about the people around them: no matter how much wealth they possessed, they were not happy. This observation was the beginning of their quest.

Sister X continues:

My family was Buddhist. I sometimes went to the temple with my grandmother, but I could not find answers there to the questions which were growing in me.

Then I made a trip to the Montreal area, where Thay was giving a talk. I didn't know who he was, but I listened to him with an open mind. I saw immediately that he was a man of simplicity, speaking of things which concerned people's daily lives. I went to the mountains where he was giving a retreat. There, I learned for the first time to sit, to walk, to eat, and to wash dishes in full consciousness. It was so simple. I saw that in all my nineteen years, I had never really lived. Then I asked myself whether I really wanted to return to a life of agitation, consumerism, and scattering my energy in all directions, or whether I would simply live my life in the present.

Everything changed for me. I began to have a real relationship with my parents. I studied at the university for three years, became an engineer, and found a well-paid job. I was able to spend money as I pleased, but it brought me little satisfaction.

Then I came here. My plan was to stay for two weeks, but it turned into six months. finally, I was ordained in 1994.

I know my weaknesses. I know I'm still unsteady, like a little stone easily dislodged by accident, yet I accept myself as I am. I'm happy, because I'm finally able to be myself.

The other two Sisters also told us how moved they were by their first meeting with Thich Nhat Hanh. All of them were overwhelmed by his simple presence, together with the lucidity and practicality of his teaching.

When we asked Sister Z, whether, at her young age, she has ever felt a bit frightened at the prospect of spending her entire life as a nun, she answers: "Not at all. If anything, I am concerned that one life might not be long enough to develop my practice. There are so many things in me which are in need of transformation."

These women's Vietnamese background meant they were already familiar with Buddhism. We wondered how it might be for some of the French nuns. We spoke with Carole, twenty-three years old, born and raised in a very Catholic French provincial family. When she was required to write a paper for a philosophy class, she chose the subject of Buddhism, without really knowing why. Among other things, this led her to read *Learning True Love*, by Sister Chan Khong. This book inspired her to make a visit to Plum Village:

> *I was especially impressed by how people here behaved towards me, a total stranger to their community. They welcomed me with such smiles, and invited me to eat with them. I felt unconditional love, and this was just what I needed. I returned the following summer to help take care of children during a retreat. Then three years passed before I finally returned. I thought I would go for just two weeks—but I'm still here! I felt that this was my path, and that I had no choice but to honor it. I told myself: "You must stay here if you want to grow."*

> *I was a person full of conflicts. I saw that by making peace with myself, I could create a little more peace in the world. It's as simple as that. And well worth whatever I have to give up in order to achieve it.*

Patricia, forty-two, arrived here by a more convoluted path. A tall, exuberant woman with a love of laughter, one sensed that she could naturally be a "life of the party" type of person. Yet it was also clear that she had been driven for many years by an inner calling she did not fully understand. When she was twenty, she made her first discovery of authentic spirituality by reading Krishnamurti:

> *Over twenty years later, I feel he is still with me. He was the first person to show me that I was living in a state of sleep. I love the way he peels away our layers of self-deception, without compromise.*

> *When I was young, my greatest passion was poetry. But there was no poetic dimension at all to our family*

life. All we ever talked about was work, managing
our affairs, and how important it was to make a good
living so as to be secure and independent.

She graduated from high school,[4] and studied to become
an electrician. She worked as a lighting technician in a theater
in Paris, and then for national television. This led to her
becoming a camera woman. Yet this success did nothing to
quench her growing thirst for truth. Not a person to do things
halfway, she registered for a month-long retreat at a Tibetan
Buddhist monastery, where everyone did eight or nine hours
of meditation each day.

She returned deeply changed by this experience. At work,
she was relaxed with her supervisors, whereas she had been
ill at ease with them before. Then, following a desire for an
exotic change, she moved to French Guyana, where she had
gotten a job in television. Later, she returned to France, where
she did a six-month meditation retreat at a Vipassana Buddhist
center. She visited Plum Village around this time, but had no
thought of staying there. In Paris, she explored psychotherapy,
while continuing her daily practice of meditation. She was a
seeker, exploring a number of paths for some years. One day she
remembered Plum Village, thinking of the kindness of the
community, and the poetic quality of Thay's teaching. She
resolved to do an entire year's retreat there, after which she
would return to her previous life.

That was not an easy year for me, because I have been
so free and independent for the last twenty years.
What pushes my buttons are the ritualistic ways of
doing things here—what we call "kind manners." I
realize I am one of Thay's more difficult students.
Things which come easy to others are hard for me,

especially involving ritual, which doesn't much interest me. I am not a very typical Buddhist. But when I look at myself, I see how deeply I have changed. This is encouraging to me.

I am such an individualist—it is only gradually that I have discovered the value of community, which we call the sangha.[5] The sangha is working upon me, shaping me, giving me the patience to wait for things to develop naturally in me.

It is so important to listen to ourselves, and be aware of how we are living. This is what is meant by being present to everything that is happening in us.

And again—I can't repeat it too often—in this path, the role of the sangha is crucial. Without it, nothing can be achieved.

5 ∾ The Meaning of the Sangha

The sangha. This is a phrase that often recurs in conversation here. We are reminded of Christian monasticism, which accords a similar importance to community. Thich Nhat Hanh constantly returns to this theme in his teachings, as in his books. It is related to the Buddhist doctrine of the Three Jewels: Buddha, Dharma,[6] and Sangha. When one becomes a Buddhist, one formally takes refuge in these three. According to Thay:

> *A Vietnamese proverb says that if a tiger comes down from its mountain, it will be killed by humans. This also applies to practitioners. If they abandon the sangha they will be lost, for the conditions of life in the world will sooner or later drag them back into forgetfulness and sleep. If they are to resist this current, they must rely on the bastion of protection which is the sangha.*

The spiritual path is not easy. We all know this. We have such a stubborn tendency to battle against our suffering, and against our problems. Instead, we must learn the practice of embracing our suffering with great kindness. But this goes against our deepest conditioning, and if we try to go this road alone, we sooner or later drift into forgetfulness of the practice. In an authentic spiritual community, however, there is always a brother or sister who can help us return to the practice when we stray.

Physically, the Plum Village sangha is divided into three hamlets, which are a few miles apart. The upper one is for men, the lower one (also known as Loubès-Bernac) is for women, and the so-called New Hamlet (also know as Dieulivol) is for women as well. The New Hamlet also houses couples who have come for retreats or longer stays. This sangha welcomes both one-time visitors and those who return periodically to renew their practice.

Thay recommends returning to one's primary sangha at difficult times, since it is a place of refuge and protection. He placed great emphasis on this during our retreat.

> *Sometimes you lose your balance in daily life. You may feel you are cracking under the strain, that you can't go on any longer, that you are no longer able to deal with your problems. If you have a friend who understands you, and who is both grounded and free, then they can be of great help. You should not hesitate to go to such a friend, sit down with them, and begin to breathe freely with them. Then you will recover your balance. Of course you can't always be with your friend, but you can take advantage of their simple presence to recover your balance.*

> *The same thing is true of the sangha. When you are here, you can take full advantage of the group energy to restore and stabilize your balance, and return home renewed. You can join your own energy of full consciousness with that of the sangha. This will give you freedom from fear. I take refuge in the sangha—this is not some declaration of belief, it is a daily practice.*

As for myself, I must take refuge in the sangha if I am to teach the dharma. I need the sangha to sustain me. It gives me great energy, support, and joy.

A teacher without a sangha is like a musician without an instrument. The sangha encourages us to develop our strengths so as to transform our weaknesses. This way which we are practicing together is a tradition which goes back 2,600 years.

This means that all practitioners, not just monks, are advised to turn to the sangha in moments of difficulty. But the sangha is also much more than this. It is an incredibly powerful source of collective energy. We can see this in action when we go from meditating alone (which is of course an indispensable practice) to meditating with a group of fellow practitioners. With even ten people (to say nothing of a hundred), we can feel a remarkable heightening of energy, available to all who come into contact with it. Who can find limits to this transformative energy? At the very least, we can say that those who are changed by it are a kind of medicine for the planet and for humanity. They radiate the energy of full consciousness, which generates understanding, compassion, and unconditional love.

In each of the three monasteries at Plum Village there is a bulletin board with a map showing locations and addresses of other sanghas. Thich Nhat Hanh is a strong advocate of people founding their own new sanghas. "Building a sangha is the noblest task human beings can undertake," he says. He recommends establishing a central place of meeting and practice for people who live in the same town, if possible. If not, then practitioners can meet at each other's houses. In any case, the aim is to meet regularly, and, as often as possible, to spend an entire day together practicing full consciousness. This is far more effective than everyone practicing separately in their own homes. In this way people can help each other, and their individual practices become all the stronger for it. In large cities, it may also be practical to establish specialized sanghas. For example, doctors or teachers may want to meet together to share the special problems they encounter in their work.

Even a family can be a sangha. Thay maintains that children are quite capable of living in full consciousness, and practicing sitting and walking meditation. This would seem to be borne out by the quality of awareness we have observed in the children around him, especially during certain walking meditations.

However, he warns against some people's tendency to run to the sangha when things go wrong, and to forget it when things go well. On the contrary, we should practice with special ardor during happy periods. This will help us all the more when we encounter suffering.

> *We know that rainy days are not the time to dry out the firewood. We have to wait until the sun is shining. When you can breathe deeply and smile, when you feel that your life is on track, this is the golden opportunity to practice the energy of full consciousness. These are your sunny days. One day it will rain, and you will need dry wood to keep warm.*

According to Sister Chan Khong, the sangha is as important as the teacher. Certainly he or she is the guide, but the teaching is enriched by the disciples' practice and by their experiences, including their problems and difficulties.

> *When we live together, we share deeply. We work together, and we progress together. The richer we*

become in this, the greater the river which carries us into the divine ocean of understanding, happiness, and love.

Every community requires some form of leadership, and each of the three hamlets at Plum Village has its abbot or abbess. At the Lower Hamlet at Loubès-Bernac, the abbess is a young woman named Gina. If we had to choose one word to describe the overall impression she makes, it would be *composure.* A quality of calm equanimity pervades her gestures, her walk, and her way of speaking. Sister Gina seems to embody the energy of full consciousness which we are seeking to cultivate in ourselves.

Plum Village is her home, yet she often travels. When we first met her, she had just returned from Germany. On our next visit, she was away in Israel, leading a meditation retreat. She tells us later how the growing thirst for peace there has led the Israeli sangha to increase its retreats to twice a year. These are attracting increasing numbers of people, including Palestinians as well as Israelis.

Her status as abbess in no way exempts her from working alongside the others, cooking, washing dishes, or laboring in the garden. Highly skilled in techniques of organic gardening, one of her favorite jobs is planting starts for rows of lettuce.

I grew up in the Netherlands. My father was Dutch, my mother Irish. When I was seven years old, I already wanted to be a nun—Catholic of course, since that was the only religion I knew.

My mother was a true Christian, who taught us that love was more important than going to mass every Sunday. I remember some Sunday mornings when the rest of us wanted to skip church and go swimming, she would tell us: "Go ahead and swim. I'll go to church for everyone." She was not saying this to make us feel guilty or wrong in any way. Without knowing it, she was already living the truth of inter-being which we try to practice here. She was always reminding us that we should love our neighbors as ourselves.

So I had this desire to become a nun. However, when I was twelve years old, I began to really observe the people around me. I saw that the priests and nuns I encountered were not really living the life to which I aspired. Already, I had high standards in my faith.

I was often alone, but I never felt lonely. I felt God was always by my side, especially during the endless walks I used to take in the woods near where we lived.

One day during our catechism lesson, the teacher asked each of us to describe God. When my turn came, I said "But I could never describe God! I would have to describe the whole universe, and I don't have enough words for that." The teacher's reaction was to declare that I was not a good Catholic.

Ever since childhood I have felt this Presence. Of course I could never explain it. Actually, many children have this experience.

My mother also practiced yoga and meditation. When I watched her, I thought: this is what I am looking for, deep down.

With such a deeply religious nature, it is not surprising that, barely out of adolescence, Gina encountered a spiritual teacher. He was very eclectic, and taught Christian prayer, Hindu mantras, and Zen meditation. One day this man told her, "In Japan there are masters of meditation who never think at all."

"Never think at all ...!" This phrase deeply impressed her, for it seemed to be the key to something of great significance. For one thing, it seemed related to a physical symptom of hers: for years she had suffered from excruciating migraine headaches, and had noticed that the pain diminished greatly when her mind was free of thoughts. She decided she must study with these masters.

Gina was 27 years old when she was finally able to go to Japan. She was overwhelmed by what she found there:

> I went to several monasteries. To find myself there, among the monks, practicing meditation in an 800-year-old monastery ... it was beyond words. I was so carried away by this energy, that all I had to do was sit on a cushion, and I would enter instantaneously into a meditative state. In 1985, during one of several return visits to Japan, I was staying in a temple in the mountains. The master there was a man of 73, in whom I felt total confidence. After three or four days, I asked him if he would accept me as a student, and he agreed. I stayed with him for three years. As time went on, I gradually began to realize many things. One of them was that my deepest search had always been for a contemplative life. If my biographical circumstances had been a little different, I might well have found this in Europe, among the Benedictines or Cistercians.

Visa problems forced her to leave Japan after three years. She visited Taiwan, where she met a spiritual teacher who asked her what she had learned in Japan. "At that time," she says, "I thought I knew something. But now I have learned that I know nothing."

Not long after her return to Europe, she heard about Plum Village. She came for a 21-day retreat, and is still there ten years later. When she decided to formally become a student of Thich Nhat Hanh, she had to first ask for her Japanese teacher's blessing. She went to Japan, and found him in the hospital.

> As soon as I walked into his room, he asked me: "Are you now able to teach the five Precepts of Full Consciousness?" When I answered yes, he said, "Very well. Now, let's have some tea." This short exchange had sufficed for him to see that I was ready to teach, and to express his acceptance of the fact that permission to teach had first come from someone else. I was very touched.

> He died in 1997. I was absent from Plum Village when the news arrived, so I found out too late to attend his funeral in Japan. They also held a large celebration to mark the traditional passage of 49 days following his passing. By that time, we were into our winter retreat, and I was unable to leave the monastery. I asked Thay if we could hold a ceremony here, and he agreed. He wrote some sacred calligraphy in Chinese for the occasion, which we placed on an altar, along with a photograph of my departed teacher. Thay then had me follow him to the altar, and he reached down and touched the Earth three times. This gesture

*moved me deeply, and in that moment I sensed that
my original teacher was very happy that Thay was
my spiritual guide.*

We asked her what it meant, in the light of her own spiritual
quest, for her to now be playing the role of abbess. She took a
long moment to reply.

*I think this role means different things for different
people. My primary concern is community life, which
is far more important to me than Buddhist studies,
for example. Community life is something that is practiced every minute of the day. Why? Because in every
minute I must face my own ability—or inability—to
love. By now I am always able to sense and know
whether I have it or not. And I know that my path is to
have it.*

*When I was eighteen years old, my friends and I
would talk about love and marriage. I would always
say that I couldn't imagine loving only one person. I
wanted to love everyone, like Jesus Christ. This is still
my path today.*

*Right now I'm responsible for those who live here,
and also for visitors. If I am to develop and manifest
this love, I must be able to recognize what their needs
are. My job is to assist them in developing their
strengths and transforming their weaknesses. And I
can succeed in this only if I am able to develop and
transform these in myself.*

*When I accept a weakness in myself, I offer it the
possibility of becoming a strength. This is something
very concrete, and can be practiced at every moment. In*

fact, this is what spiritual practice really is. It is not feeling guilty for your weaknesses, it is realizing that at every instant, you can simply return to your true nature. The door is always open.

Father Philippe, a priest at the nearby Orthodox monastery of Sainte-Croix, came here and spoke to us once. He said, "We are here on Earth to learn to love." I am in total agreement with that, as I am with the way the great abbesses and abbots of the Christian tradition played their roles.

It has been my experience that living in full consciousness can be learned. It can become a habit, replacing the habit of unconsciousness. For example, I can now recognize whether I am being fully present or not. From time to time I see that I am not. And I simply think: "Return." And I do return—over and over, however many times it takes. When I see I am not living in the present, I have a choice: I can either continue with my daydreaming, out of touch with my own body, or I can simply return. And I discover that with a little training, this return becomes progressively easier. Then I can be conscious for much longer periods, and my mind becomes lighter and lighter. This is especially effortless for me on Lazy Days.

6 ∾ *Lazy Days and New Beginnings*

Lazy Day. This is an important tradition at Plum Village. The name would seem to contradict the image of a serious, traditional monastery—which Plum Village undoubtedly is. Yet it is a direct application of one of Thich Nhat Hanh's teachings. During his first visit to the West long ago, he was immediately struck by the feverish pace of activity, with people in cities hurrying everywhere. More recently, calendars full of appointments have become a virtual fetish. People seem afraid of empty time, and the less they have to work, the more they obsessively fill it up with distractions such as television, and shallow amusements.

In his book *La sérénité de l'instant*, he writes:

> *In the West, we are completely driven by our goals. We want to know where we are going, and we mobilize all our energy to get there. This attitude can certainly be useful, but it often makes us forget to enjoy ourselves along the way.*

> *There is a term in Buddhism which signifies absence of wish, or absence of goal. This refers to a state in which it is meaningless to run after some object of desire, because everything is already here, in oneself. When we practice walking meditation, we are not*

trying to get anywhere. We are satisfied with just walking, in peace and joy. When we think constantly about the future, about what we are trying to accomplish, we go astray.

Often we tell ourselves, "Don't just sit there—do something!" In fact, the practice of awareness brings us a startling discovery: perhaps real usefulness is elsewhere. Perhaps we should instead tell ourselves: "Don't just do something—sit there!"

We must learn to stop from time to time, if we are to see more clearly. At first this stopping may seem to be a kind of resistance to modern life, but this is not so. This practice is not a mere reaction, it is exercising our capacity to not be in a hurry. Its object is not to escape from life, but to live it fully, and to prove that the happiness of being alive is possible both today and in the future.

At Plum Village, Monday is Lazy Day. There is no structure, or work, except for meals. Otherwise, everyone is free to follow their own rhythm, getting up as late as they please, sleeping when they like, taking walks, or doing nothing. Even work is allowed, provided the work is done for relaxation, and (inasmuch as this is possible) is not some task which the person already has to do every day.

Sister Gina tells us that the word "lazy" is deliberately provocative, a challenge to the modern fetish of busyness. Such constant occupation is merely a form of social conditioning, and not at all the virtue people suppose it to be.

Lazy days are sometimes difficult for the younger nuns. They find it hard to be thrown back on themselves like this, with no work schedule, few bells ringing,

no duties or instructions. Structured activities have
become something which they imagine they need.

When Rachel and I first experienced the lazy hours on Monday morning before lunch, we luxuriated in having nothing to do. Even the bells had been silenced. But as the day wore on, we realized that laziness, too, is a form of spiritual practice—and not so easy for many of us! Just try sometime to take an entire day off, and practice true laziness, with no obligation or structure, other than providing for your bodily needs. And don't forget that the essential thing is to *practice this laziness in full consciousness....*

The full moon and the new moon are also important rhythms of life at Plum Village. On these days, twice a month, the residents in each of the three monasteries gather round their abbot or abbess for the observance of *Beginning Anew.*

This is an especially important moment for interpersonal relationships. It is a time for members of the community to freely and publicly express their appreciation for and to each other. It is also a time for honest examination of one's conscience regarding relations with others. This is quite similar to practices in many Christian communities, but without any trace of guilt feelings—neither harboring them in oneself, nor provoking them in others.

first, the Buddhist precepts are read aloud. A pause follows each precept, when anyone who wishes to make a comment or express a feeling may do so. However, this is not a discussion. The aim is for everyone to listen deeply, and in full consciousness, to these comments, feelings, or questions.

Then comes the moment called "watering the flowers," when people may publicly express feelings of gratitude directly to other members of the community. Very often it will be for something another person has done. This could be some little service, a kindness, or almost anything. It could even be gratefulness for an individual's especially ardent practice: "Thank you for your practice, because I know it benefits me, too."

Regrets may also be expressed at this time. For example, "Last week you asked me to do something, and I replied unkindly. I regret this." But again, there is no discussion. It is a simple acknowledgment, with no indulgence in guilt or reassurance.

Gina has a good deal to say about Beginning Anew:

> *This practice requires deep listening and loving kindness in one's speech. In ordinary life, when someone thanks us for something, we say "no problem," or (in French) "it was nothing." Here, even though we may accept it in silence, we welcome this gratitude as if a flower were being offered to us. It is not "nothing"! And when we express a regret, the person to whom it is offered accepts it in silence, without replying.*

Of course things do not always happen so smoothly in this, or any other community. Sometimes resentments develop, and wounds that do not heal so quickly. It may happen that a person to whom we make a request or a complaint refuses to accept it. At Plum Village, everyone has a right to express their hurt over such a rejection—but *never in the heat of the moment*. We must wait until our anger has fully subsided. As Sister Gina says:

> *We must take care of our own anger or remorse before we speak. Then, when the moment arrives, we will be able to find words that are not hurtful. When things are calm, we can meet with the other person. The conversation might begin something like this: "I could be mistaken, but I had the feeling that you said*

those words to me in a rather unkind way, and I felt hurt by it." The other listens. Occasionally this may involve a deep wound, because an extremely sensitive spot has been touched. In this case, the wounded person must look deep within, so as to see whether there might be a grain of truth in what the other person has said. But in order to do this, compassion for oneself is essential. Otherwise, such a truth will be extremely hard to accept or digest. Lack of self-compassion leads to defensiveness and resentment towards the other. This makes it difficult to restore harmony.

We must understand that it is our conditioning that makes us the way we are. We were born in a certain kind of family and social environment, subject to the conditioning of parents, siblings, peers, teachers—all of them reacting to their conditioning as well. Once we really see this, we can begin to have compassion for ourselves, and not be threatened by critical remarks from others.

Such confrontations rarely do harm, and their main effect in a community is to bring people closer together in mutual understanding. Years of these Beginning Anew sessions have taught us how amazingly interconnected we all are. What I say influences others, and what others say influences me. As we realize this, we gradually learn to be truly free together. This is a very beautiful thing—it's what the value of community is really all about.

A special practice of Beginning Anew is reserved for couples who reside at the New Hamlet. Sister Chan Khong, one of

Thay's oldest dharma companions, is the abbess here. She modestly describes herself as "Thay's secretary," but she is much more than this. She has long taken a special interest in the problems and practices relevant to couples, and many who have come here have been helped by her. We were surprised and fascinated to hear this venerable Buddhist nun speak, in her own robust and inimitable way, about falling in love:

> When you fall in love with someone, the "thunder-bolt" sometimes has a simple explanation: when you were a small child, your mother was sometimes very nervous and disturbed. Then your favorite aunt came to visit. She had blue eyes and blond hair, was a very sweet person, and treated you with great affection and kindness. This made a profound impression, and caused a flowering of love and tenderness in you.

> Then you forget all this as you grow up and go through adolescence. One day you meet a girl with blond hair and blue eyes like your aunt, and you think: "This is my soul-mate, the woman I have been waiting for." You fall in love with each other, have an affair, and start living together. After awhile, you begin to notice that she is not always the wonderful creature you thought and dreamed she was. Little conflicts begin to appear, and then wounds.

> After three months or three years, you feel like fleeing this relationship. If you're a doctor, you may find good reasons to spend a lot more time taking care of your patients, instead of going home and listening to complaints. If you're a writer, you may plunge into your work, accepting so many commitments that you no

longer have time to discuss things at home. Thay often says that work can be an escape from the problems of life.

There is a special Beginning Anew practice for couples who may be experiencing some disenchantment. We try to help them see that they may be harboring a mistaken image of their partner. The true nature of this other person has not been discovered. Granted, this woman may be quite different from the lovely dream you once thought she was. And this man may be very far from the daddy you wish you had. But this other person is still who they are, a marvelous reality in their own true nature. They can still bring you a joy which you have yet to discover.

What can we do to help such a couple discover this reality? first, we suggest that from now on, they do a Beginning Anew session every week, instead of every two weeks. If you can find the time to do the shopping, the housework, and wash your car, why can't you find the time once a week to renew your love? What a shame, to claim you don't have time for this! It's so important! Thay suggests choosing a certain day of the week—Friday is best for most people, because then you'll have the whole weekend to enjoy afterward. If you've had any problems during the week, if you have spoken unpleasantly to each other, or if you have a complaint to make, I beg you—wait until Friday! When something unpleasant happens during the week, try to avoid retorting or discussing it right away. This is not the best time to deal with the problem. You are still in the heat of reaction, frustration, or resentment. Take the time to find your calm, to allow refreshing peace and kindness to return to your heart.

Then, when Friday evening comes, you begin by taking a flower and passing it back and forth to each other. Only the person holding the flower has the right to speak. They may speak as long as they like, with no interruption by the other allowed. first, look at the flower, smell it, and let yourself be touched by its beautiful, peaceful being. You should begin the session by saying positive things. For example, "You know, it was really wonderful of you to spend all that time with my mother, especially when you had so much work to do." It is very important to begin this practice with true and sincere appreciation for each other. This will create an atmosphere in which problems have the best chance of being solved.

Then, and only then, express your regrets for your own behavior—all the regrets accumulated over the week. For example, "You were so beautiful in your new dress, and I didn't even say anything. I forgot to tell you how wonderful you are," or "I forgot to thank you for doing that chore I was supposed to do."

Now we arrive at the third part, and of course it is the most delicate and difficult. Here, we express not only our regret, but our discontent. It is essential to remain calm, listening to the other without interrupting, and both of you resisting the temptation to forget the flower and get into a discussion. This goes against our habits, but with a little practice, it can be learned. "You said something last Tuesday that really bothered me. I feel hurt, I can't understand. Please explain why you said that." And pass the flower to the other. Sometimes this will be enough to elicit an explanation which brings immediate understanding and forgiveness, resolving the problem.

Here is an example which happened to a couple I know. These young lovers went on a picnic. The woman was not hungry. She ate the center part of her sandwich, and threw the rest in the garbage. She was shocked at the angry and sullen reaction of her partner. She couldn't understand why he was so upset about throwing away a little bread. She thought him miserly, and felt angry in her turn.

But they refrained from getting into an argument about it. Fortunately, they had been introduced to the practice of Beginning Anew. Two days later, on Friday evening, they began the ritual, and at length came to this incident. It was she who first spoke of it: "Do you remember how happy we were the day we went on our picnic? Then I threw away a little bread because I wasn't hungry, and I felt that you looked at me as if I was a criminal. Please explain this, I don't understand."

Now, this young man was Vietnamese. His family had led a comfortable life when he was very young—his father was a military doctor, and his grandfather had also been a doctor. When the communists arrived, they arrested his father and sent him to a "re-education" camp. Now, for the first time, he told his young wife the rest of the story:

"Our house was confiscated, and our family sent to the countryside. We lived in misery, and there were *days when we had nothing at all to eat. You see, when the war ended, we had no money left at all. Like other educated families in the South, we had put our money in the bank. This turned out to be a disaster. We were totally destitute. We would have done better to hide a little gold, like some of the simple peasants did. When my father was finally released from the camp, he told us that he had been so hungry there that he would sometimes scavenge a few grains of rice he found lying about, just to have a bite to eat that day.*

"Since you have never known this kind of lack, throwing away a piece of bread seems normal to you. But for us, a piece of bread was sacred. We were very economical, and never threw things away if we could help it."

Now the young woman understood, and felt amazement and love for him. It was her understanding that changed things—without understanding, she would have continued to feel hurt instead of love. This is a good example of how we practice Beginning Anew for couples. In this way, they can go beyond just being in love, and learn true love for each other. They can understand what is really behind each other's behavior, and become as one. This can only happen in joy, never in exasperation. The golden rule to follow here is to refrain from speaking until we are calm. It is essential to avoid discussions or arguments which take place in the heat of reaction.

Holding the flower while you speak not only slows both of you down, it also reminds you of the freshness, beauty, and vitality of the Buddha-nature in everything.

However, just because you hold the flower does not give you the right to say hurtful things. If someone feels that the person holding the flower is being aggressive, it is best to simply say "I'd like to stop now." In such a case, you will have to wait awhile longer before trying again.

7 ∾ *Christian Buddhists and Buddhist Christians*

*W*e remember Martina from the ordination ceremony. This tall young German woman stood out among the other postulants, most of whom were Vietnamese. Her parents were seated close by, and her father took many photographs, as if to document the occasion.

She is twenty-nine years old, and has been at Plum Village for a year and a half. Her story is a good example of the bridges that are now being built between Buddhism and Christianity. An only child, she is quite aware of having had a privileged life, materially speaking. In spite of her family's easy circumstances, she felt a void in herself which nothing could fill. Prone to self-perfectionism, she was never satisfied. She had a great need to look deeper into things, but did not know how. By the time she was nineteen, she felt as if she had fallen into a dark hole.

Driven by her demanding nature, and being a German Protestant, she decided to study theology. These studies fascinated her, and she worked hard at them for years. After graduate work and advanced diplomas, she was on the verge of becoming a pastor. But she knew that something was still lacking, and had been since the beginning of her theological studies. They seemed overly intellectual, and lacking in a crucial element which she most needed: practice.

Only a few months before she was to be assigned to a parish, she felt a need to explore different practices, and visited several monasteries, doing short retreats. In Switzerland, she happened to see a film about Thich Nhat Hanh and Plum Village. She felt that this would be just the place for her to do some deep practice of contemplation before assuming her new responsibilities. Hopping on her motorcycle, she arrived there in time to do a three-week retreat.

During the last days of her stay there, a thought kept recurring over and over: why not stay at Plum Village for a much longer time? After her return home, and in the midst of all her preparations for her new life, this thought continued to haunt her. About four weeks later, a day came when she suddenly realized that she was free. She had not yet received any commission, and had no responsibilities toward any parish. On the spot, she resolved to leave it all. Selling her motorcycle and moving out of her apartment, she returned to Plum Village to stay.

She felt she had discovered her spiritual home. The practice, the environment, Thay's teaching—she felt permeated by these, and had no doubt that she had done the right thing.

However, as time went on, she realized that she did not really feel like a Buddhist, and had no desire to become one.

> Before I requested to be ordained here, I studied the five Precepts of Full Consciousness. Paradoxically, it was then that I realized that I would never be a Buddhist. Switching religions made no sense to me. I saw that my roots were Christian, and that the real goal of my work here was to deepen them. When I am speaking with Buddhists, I speak a Buddhist language. But when I meet visitors who come here from outside, I am happy to speak to them in a language they understand—

in most cases, a Christian one. But I stay here because of the depth of inquiry and practice, which I have not found elsewhere. It is not so important whether your language is that of Nirvana, the Kingdom of God, full consciousness, the sangha, or the Holy Spirit ... these are all just different approaches to the same Reality.

During my studies of Christian theology, I was told that what set us apart from all other religions was that Jesus Christ was the only Son of God. I could not accept that dogma then, and I cannot accept it now. It is one of those later doctrines fabricated by the Church. I find such dogmas unimportant, and a poor way of teaching Christianity. What is really important in any religion is to experience the presence of God, to live our lives in such a way that this experience is always close to us. This is the truly wondrous life. Whether we call ourselves Christians, Buddhists, Hindus, or Moslems, I believe that we are all the sons and daughters of God. In this light, how can we possibly take anyone seriously who goes around saying things like, "If you don't believe in such-and-such, you are a child of Satan, not of God."

We must go beyond words and formulas. It doesn't bother me at all to be living two religions at once. My strong practice of Buddhism has taught me a lot about Christianity. They work very well together. I am learning so much by going back and forth between them. It is a school in itself.

The emphasis at Plum Village is on practice, which is what I need. But I can also practice Christian prayer here. I simply let go of any ideas which would interfere with this.

I was struck by something I once heard Thay say to a Vietnamese nun from the U.S.: "Since you are both Vietnamese and American, you can be a bridge between the two." I hope that I will someday be a kind of bridge between Buddhism and Christianity.

Buddhists have an attitude towards the Buddha which is full of veneration and love. Christians have a tendency to worship a Being which is beyond themselves. Buddhists have a tendency to first go within, believing that the world and others are to be found there. Christians tend to look for God first in others and in the world, and thereby discover their own depths. These two approaches are both right, and sooner or later arrive at the same truth. Beyond all our differences, we can agree that God, or Buddha-nature, is everywhere, within and without. The rest is just vocabulary. Ultimately, it is the Experience that counts.

This way of thinking is not just something peculiar to Marina. It is very much in harmony with Thich Nhat Hanh's own teaching. As a young man, he had to overcome considerable obstacles in order arrive at an appreciation and love for the Christ and for Christians. Catholic missionaries did little to endear themselves to most Vietnamese. Ngo Dinh Diem, the South Vietnamese president installed by the Americans, was a Roman Catholic. As the war grew worse, he issued an edict forbidding the celebration of Wesak, the most important Buddhist holiday.

It was only later that Thay encountered true Christians. Two of the most famous of were Thomas Merton and Martin Luther King. He speaks with great admiration of them as human beings and as spiritual teachers. He also became friends with Daniel Berrigan, the Jesuit priest who later made headlines in America for his acts of resistance to the war, leading to a long imprisonment.

Through the years, Thay has not only come to respect Christianity, but in a sense to embrace it. On his personal altar at his small residence just outside the hamlets, he has placed images of Christ and of Buddha. "Every time I light a stick of incense, I feel linked to both of them," he says. "They are my spiritual ancestors."

He has never asked any disciple of his to convert to Buddhism. Quite the contrary. Once a non-Buddhist student has completed their study of the five Precepts of Full Consciousness, and the Three Jewels, he tells them: "And now I hope that you will return to your original tradition and shed light upon the jewels that are already there. I ask you to practice these jewels as you have learned them here, or as they are practiced in your original tradition."

This ecumenical approach comes to full fruition in his book, *Living Buddha, Living Christ*.

> *The Living Christ is the Christ of love. At every instant, he emanates only love. When the Church shows understanding, tolerance, and kindness, then Jesus is there. Christians must help Jesus Christ to manifest through their way of life, demonstrating to everyone around them that love, understanding, and tolerance are possible. It is not through sermons and books that we will bring this about, but through our way of being in the world. In Buddhism, we also say that the living*

Buddha, teacher of love and compassion, must manifest through the way we live.

Thanks to so many generations of Buddhist and Christian practitioners, the energy of Buddha and the energy of Jesus Christ are still with us. We can touch the living Buddha, we can touch the living Christ. Our knowledge that our own body is the continuation of the body of Buddha, and that it is part of the mystical body of Christ, is a wonderful means for helping both Buddha and Christ to continue their work here and now.

One of the most interesting reflections in this book originated in a conversation with a Florentine priest, whom Thay asked about the meaning of the Holy Spirit.

He told me: "The Holy Spirit is the energy sent by God." This answer pleased me immensely, because it confirmed my intuition that the surest way to get in touch with the Trinity is through the door of the Holy Spirit. For me, what we call full consciousness *is very close to the Holy Spirit. Both are vehicles of healing.*

When the Holy Spirit descended upon Jesus in the form of a dove, it filled him to his depths, and Jesus then became a revealer of the Holy Spirit's manifestations. He healed everything he touched, and the Holy Spirit in him gave him the power to transform many people. All schools of Christianity are in agreement about this.

I then told the monk that I felt that we all have the seed of the Holy Spirit in us—the capacity to heal, to

love, and to transform. By touching this seed, we are
able to touch God the Father and God the Son.

It is not surprising that many Christians are attracted to Plum Village. They have always felt at ease there, recognized and appreciated in their faith. Over the years, this has led to the seemingly paradoxical situation of a Buddhist monastery which includes a significant number of monks and nuns who are Christian, and recognized as such by the community.

After hearing Marina's story, we wanted to follow this thread further by speaking with Sister Elizabeth. We were told that her passion for inter-religious harmony had led her to consider herself both fully Buddhist and fully Christian. Her somewhat delicate, fragile appearance belied the combination of strength and kindness we saw in her eyes. It was clear from the start that her childhood was one which very much favored religious tolerance and understanding:

> *I was born in Morocco. We moved to Marrakesh, where my father's work took him. My parents and grandparents were very devout Christians, and also quite open-minded.*
>
> *When I first asked my mother about the Muezzin's call to prayer, she told me, "My dear, there are men and women out there who are following that voice to a place of prayer, but it is not a church. They are following the call of God, though they call him by a different name in this country. Often you will see people here prostrating themselves on the ground. You must have great respect for this, for it is how they worship." Later, when we happened to pass through the Jewish quarter, we saw some men with curly sideburns*

and kipas (yarmulkes) on their heads. She explained to me that we should see these men as our brothers, because they devoted their whole lives to God.

My parents' openness to other religions did not make them any less profoundly Christian. They often told me that there was a spark of God to be found in every person and in everything. There was nothing from which it was absent, and all that I saw was a reflection of the Divine.

I was given these discoveries like a gift of grace. When I think of it, I find it marvelous that when we moved to Mogador, our house turned out to be the same one where Father Foucauld[7] had lived. When I was six years old, I took what was then called "private communion." It was an experience full of love for me. My parents taught us our catechism at home, and they talked constantly about Saint Francis of Assisi and Saint Therese of Lisieux. I was surrounded by an atmosphere full of love.

Our house in Marrakesh was in an Arab quarter. It was not the same as it is now. Then, there was a lot of misery to be seen: blind people, crippled people, and small children whose constantly runny eyes were covered with flies. I felt very fortunate, and knew that I should do as my mother did, and use this to help the most unhappy people.

I had a great desire to be a nun, but I fell in love with a man I met, and we got married. We had two children who are grown now—one of them celebrated her thirtieth birthday on January 1, 2000.

My husband was totally uninterested in any of the outer manifestations of religion, so I no longer practiced as most Christians do. I would occasionally attend mass, but mostly for weddings, baptisms, or funerals. But even then, I used these occasions to take communion with great fervor.

In spite of this, she felt that she was on a profound and very demanding quest. She was not fully aware of it, but she was really looking for a spiritual teacher. She encountered disciples of various teachers, but never felt that any of them were right for her. But her search became more insistent, and she was full of a multitude of deep questions. Then she happened to speak with a Vietnamese doctor who was an acupuncturist. He spoke with engaging enthusiasm about his teacher, Thich Nhat Hanh. Two months later, in the city of Lyon, she attended a talk by him.

As I left after the talk, the thought crossed my mind that his teaching was a rather simple and obvious one. But by the time I reached home, I found myself telling my husband and children that I felt as if I had met Saint Francis of Assisi. I had only seen Thay from a distance, and for a short time. But somehow I realized that I would never have another teacher—he was the one I had been waiting for.

Naturally, I went to Plum Village as soon as I could. This was in 1987, when it was first opening. In those early days, there were only a few of us around Thay. During my first stay, I had the good fortune to have a private interview with him. I was Christian then, and still am now. But I knew that this religion, in the forms available to me, had never offered me the skills to really transform myself: to no longer be possessed by anger, to become a truly loving person. Thay was able to give me these skills.

Ten years after my first encounter with Thich Nhat Hanh, my husband left me. We had been married for thirty-one years, and engaged for four. Of course this caused me great pain. But I also realized that all the years of this very active family and professional life were beginning to recede as if the clock was turning back, and that my old, half-forgotten desire to be a nun had re-emerged in a very natural way. I knew that no Catholic convent would accept a divorced woman, no matter what the circumstances of the divorce. But this was moot in any case, for I knew that my place was with Thay. He welcomed me to Plum Village, and I have been very happy ever since.

What is so wonderful and appropriate for me, is that his teaching is totally practice-oriented. In those days I was a physical therapist, working with terminally ill people at a geriatric hospital in the city of St-Etienne. In that environment, I witnessed the extraordinary effects of the practice of full consciousness. This was confirmed by the doctors and nurses who worked with me. Even with the most damaged patients, I always tried to practice full consciousness. This meant not only being aware of the needs and projections of the patients, but of the other personnel as well. It meant being aware of the suffering, but also of all the happiness which was around us. The truth is that just by being fully conscious ourselves, we can help others, even when they are very sick, to discover the beauty which surrounds and permeates their being. In that hospital, we did some amazing guided meditations.

For example, we learned that patients were entirely capable of becoming conscious that the clean sheets they were lying on were not just something to be taken for granted, but the outcome of a vast chain of events. This included not only the personnel who changed and cleaned the sheets—it went all the way back to the manufacture of the sheet, the cotton fields, the many people who played their roles in the transformation of plant into sheet, the soil, the air, the rain, and the sun. It may seem a little bizarre at first, but this meditation on clean sheets is a very effective means of bringing patients out of their stupor and back into the heart of life. It teaches them that they do not have to continue feeling separate in their suffering, that they can learn to feel at one with their surroundings, starting with the hospital personnel, the laundry workers, and extending without boundaries in space or time. This is extremely important, for the greatest source of suffering of these people is the feeling of being separate and alone on their sickbed. As soon as they begin to open and rediscover their connection to the universe, they experience happiness, no matter how serious their illness. Our general term for this type of practice was "meditation on non-loneliness." They were quite astounding. The patients who did this practice were even able to forget their suffering, at least during the meditation.

With patients who had become more or less physically helpless, I would often take their hand and breathe with them, saying in a soft voice: "Breathing in, I know I am breathing in. Breathing out, I know I am breathing out." If appropriate, this could even develop into an elaborate guided meditation, looking at the whole process of breathing, with oxygen in and carbon dioxide out, etc. Both we and the patients learned that even when you are paralyzed, you are still part of the great movement of life. Whenever possible, I complemented this meditation with a massage, which restored awareness of life and sensation to body parts which had seemed dead.

Breathing and holding the person's hand also enabled me to draw their attention back to their body. I would ask them, "How does my hand feel? Is it cool? Warm?" This helps them to get out of their head and in touch with pleasant sensations; massage is generally very pleasant, stimulating neurons and relaxing muscles. This is a very gentle type of massage which enlivens the body. It can be practiced right up to the approach of death. When possible, I invite the dying person to dwell on all the beautiful and positive things that they have done in their life, so that they can leave the body in peace. Sometimes, when appropriate, I even sing very softly at the moment of departure.

This impressive first-hand account demonstrates how universal Thich Nhat Hanh's teaching can be in application. This practice can illuminate and transform the meanings of the most varied and unexpected activities of everyday life.

After this experience, it was not surprising that Elizabeth's sense of a religious calling became so strong that she had to respond. It was not easy, because she felt herself a Christian in her deepest heart and soul. On several occasions she sought advice from Christian friends. Both a monk and a nun gave her essentially the same advice, separately: "Christianity is your path, but this man is your teacher. You must accept this." This was confirmed by Thay himself when she told him she wanted to become a Buddhist nun. He accepted her, but only on condition that she not break with her Christian roots. He also insisted that she feel free to continue to attend mass and take communion any time she felt the need.

> During my ordination ceremony, when Thay handed me my nun's robe after cutting a lock of hair, I placed it on my head and pronounced the ritual vow: "How beautiful is this nun's robe! It is the abode of all merits. I vow to wear it life after life, and bring joy to all beings." Yet after saying this, I was bothered by the question: How could I still be a true Christian and take a vow like this? Well, shortly afterward, seemingly by accident (but showing that there are no accidents), I happened to look in a book about Saint Thérèse of Lisieux. As she was dying, she said: "I go now to rejoin my Beloved. I shall beg him not to allow me to enter heaven as long there is even one suffering being in the world." This was amazing to me, because it is the same as the bodhisattva vow.[8] I felt such support coming from this little sister, whom I already loved with all my heart.

> In fact, I now see no reason why a Christian should not bow before the Buddha. Was he not a marvelous

man who devoted his whole life to helping beings who suffer? Today, he continues to bring us sustenance, but he is not God, and never said he was. It is not idolatry to bow before him. In fact, if we have lost our Christian roots, Buddha can help us to rediscover them. Thay places great emphasis on this. I am certain that if Jesus and the Buddha had met, they would have understood one another perfectly. Did they not both work for the good of humanity?

I know from my own experience that Thich Nhat Hanh's techniques have enabled me to understand and live the teachings of Jesus more deeply. He has shown me a profound inner silence. I did pray before I met him, but it was sort of like trying to communicate with someone at a noisy banquet, with too much distraction. Now the room is empty and silent.

Sister Elisabeth illustrates here the primary importance of silence in Buddhism. The Buddha was famous for his refusal to be drawn into the interminable metaphysical discussions which were so fashionable in his day. He even refused to talk about God. And every time someone tried to entice him into a discussion of God and Self, he would only say that a separate, personal God is just as illusory as a separate, personal self. Sister Elisabeth, both Buddhist and Christian, sees God as the infinite ocean of life and love which is everywhere and in everything.

It is rare in our day to hear of a mother who has lived a full family life entering a convent. Fortunately, all her relatives and friends have greatly supported her in her decision. She feels that her two children have been especially wonderful. Her son practices meditation, and she sees her daughter as a person of extraordinary maturity and clarity. Shortly after the birth of the latter's first child, when a friend congratulated her for bringing a new life into the world, she replied, "Yes, but I have also brought a new death into the world." This was not said in sadness or bitterness, but as a deep acknowledgment of the truth of impermanence, which is so fundamental to Buddhism.

She and her brother attended the ordination ceremony of their mother, and took great pleasure in the festivities which followed. A little later during this first year as a Buddhist nun, she took leave to visit her children and take communion with them.

> For me, Christianity and Buddhism both lead to the miracle which is called transformation. Jesus is Jesus and Buddha is Buddha. For me, they are distinct, yet they are not separate. They are like two beings at my side, each holding one of my hands, helping me to advance on my path.... Walking with Thay and with the sangha, I am also walking in the footsteps of Jesus.

This recalls Thich Nhat Hanh's own words in his book, *For There to Be a Future:*

> The five Precepts of Full Consciousness, as well as the Three Jewels, have their counterparts in all spiritual traditions. They arise from a source very deep within us all, and practicing them helps us to ground ourselves better in our own religious tradition. It is my hope that, after studying the five Precepts, you will return to your original tradition and bring to light the jewels which are already present there. The five Precepts are medicine for the times we live in. I urge

> *you to practice them as you have learned them here, or*
> *as they are taught in your tradition.*

What better statement of the depth and sincerity of religious tolerance and openness at Plum Village? Yet this inter-religious harmony avoids shallow eclecticism by being grounded in an authentic Buddhist tradition. The combination of rigorous practice with deep respect for other paths is a major factor in the sense of freedom and relaxation that first-time visitors report, especially those from very different traditions, or from no tradition at all.

We conclude this theme with a somewhat different story. Like most monastics, Do-ji is culturally French, but he has been a Buddhist monk for the last fifteen years. A man with a ready and infectious smile, he was born in Tlemcen, Algeria, a town which is sacred to both Moslems and Jews.

> *I have three major roots, and life has taught me that*
> *I must water them all. My original root is Christian,*
> *but I was deeply influenced by the Moslem land where*
> *I was born. And then there is Buddhism, which has*
> *transformed my life—and enabled me to get in touch*
> *with my original roots. Whatever your tradition, the*
> *deeper you go into it, the more harmony you discover*
> *with other paths, and the more extraordinary your*
> *life becomes.*

We sensed a strong, unaffected fervor in Do-ji's manner. When we alluded to it, he told us of his belief that he somehow inherited it from the sister of his grandfather, whom he only met in her old age. She lived in the original house of his paternal branch of the family in Burgundy. She was regarded as a saint by the other villagers, and made her house and her food available to the local poor, who called it "the Good Lord's house." He was only seven when she died, but he felt a deep link with her, and told a Cistercian Father about it. The priest assured him that such cases of "transmission of the heart" were well-known.

> However, my first steps on the real road home began when I was able to listen to that voice deep inside me. There comes a time when you just can't continue doing what your friends and society think you should do. Suddenly you hear that voice, and you say: "There! That's my way." This is where the road home really begins. I had long believed that my spiritual path began when I was ordained as a monk, but I realized later that this was not true. It began long before.

Do-ji now realizes that he has been on a path of spiritual discovery for a very long time. Yet it was only years later that he was able to recognize it as such. His early discovery of body awareness began with his passion for the art of movement, which led to a career as a professional dancer.

> The human body, the dance—or more accurately, movement itself—was my quest. I began to understand that dance is a sacred art. One day an odd and mysterious thing occurred to me: I felt that I had discovered the origin of my body movement. It was a very specific place, a spot about an inch or so below the navel. Later I learned that this was called the hara in Japanese. That same day, or shortly afterward, a friend strongly recommended that I visit a Zen center. I wasn't at all receptive to this idea, but she insisted so much that I finally went. I was lucky, because right from the start, I met teachers there who really emphasized the truth of impermanence. This made

a profound impression on me, though I knew nothing about Buddhism at the time, and wasn't much interested in it.

But the young dancer had been well-prepared for his encounter with the notion of impermanence, so difficult at first for many people, well before he began to study Buddhism. He had a dance teacher who taught impermanence in a very original way:

In order to gracefully perform the complex and strenuous movements involved in dance, you must study and practice long, intricate exercises, sequences which are often quite difficult to learn. The great originality of this teacher was that, as soon as he saw that you had begun to master a movement, he quickly switched you to something you didn't know. This was radically different from other teachers, who go along with our natural inclination to repeat what we know over and over, so as to perfect it. But not this one! He would either give you something completely different, or perhaps recapitulate what you had just learned, but only to transform it into something else. The core message of his teaching was that the mind must constantly adapt itself to change. It was thanks to his influence that I immediately resonated with the teaching of impermanence, when I began to study Buddhism.

In fact, his resonance with Buddhism itself was so powerful that he soon left for Japan. He was ordained as a monk, and spent nine years there, studying with a Zen master. Then he returned to France for a month-long visit with his family. Not long after his arrival, a Buddhist friend telephoned him, saying, "I'm living at a place called Plum Village, and there is a most extraordinary teacher here. You must come for a visit." At first this seemed quite absurd to him: here he was living as a Zen monk at a monastery in Japan, and with only a precious month's vacation to visit his family, this friend wanted him to spend part of it in a Zen monastery in France! But something in her tone convinced him to go anyway.

> As soon as I arrived here and met Thay, my doubts fell away and I saw everything with perfect clarity. I had met many Zen masters over the last nine years, and had experienced many teachings, ceremonies, and practices. Here, I knew immediately that I was in the presence of a very great teacher. I saw that he had accomplished the work that I most needed to do. He was utterly simple, utterly profound, and he knew so perfectly how to walk, how to eat, how to speak, and how to sit. And incredibly, he lived in my home country, and spoke perfect French!

On returning to Japan, he asked and received his teacher's permission to take his full vows with Thay, and become his disciple. Then he returned to France ... a full circle, taking nine years to complete. At this point in his story, he broke into hearty peals of laughter. But then Do-ji is very prone to laughing, and did a lot of it during our interview. The very image of a happy, highly accomplished Zen monk.

Yet we were surprised to learn that even Do-ji had a profound Christian side, which he only discovered after meeting Thay. He had long since lost interest in Christianity, even before becoming a Buddhist. The Bible appeared to him as a book full of violence, difficult to understand, full of cryptic passages, not very interesting on the whole.

However, at Plum Village he became curious about their neighbors, the Greek Orthodox monastery of Sainte-Croix (Holy Cross). With Thay's encouragement, he began to make frequent visits there. Interested in what Do-ji had discovered, Thay invited Father Philippe, the Abbot, to speak at Plum Village in the context of ongoing ecumenical dialogues.

> *His visits had a major impact on our community. As you know, most Vietnamese have a rather narrow idea of Christianity. This is entirely understandable when you consider its role in the bloody events of their recent history, when the southern Catholic-influenced government engaged in severe repression of Buddhism. These encounters with Father Philippe showed them a radically different kind of Christianity, which both astounded and delighted them. And I was almost as surprised as the Vietnamese, because this led to my discovering a deeper way to read the Bible.*

Never a person to do things by halves, Do-ji embarked on a profound study of the Bible. This disciple of the Buddha even learned Hebrew, and developed a special enthusiasm for the book of Genesis, which he interprets as a story of the origin of his own mind, as it is here and now. Thich Nhat Hanh has never ceased to encourage him in this research.

> *As Thay often tells us, "You have treasures hidden in your original tradition." My life is now filled with the discovery of these treasures. I am infinitely grateful to Thay for this.*

8 ~ Meditation in Action

*O*ver a hundred people are walking, with exquisitely slow and deliberate paces, along the little path. They form a long, strange, uneven, silent procession which stretches out lazily into the distance on this cool spring morning. Thich Nhat Hanh leads the procession. When we catch a glimpse of his face on a turn, it is so serene, so relaxed and yet concentrated, that we feel his savoring of every movement, of his every step upon the soft, springy ground. We recall the whispered exclamation we heard the other day from a visitor: "He walks like a prince!" And indeed, this walk he practices and teaches is one of both freedom and sovereignty.

When passing farmers happen to see these bizarre, slow lines of people moving along the country paths of Plum Village, they sometimes stare, wondering what on earth its purpose is. Most passers-by shrug, and move on. But a few of the more interested neighbors know that this is *walking meditation*, one of the most important practices in this tradition. Indeed, Thay teaches that it is as important as sitting meditation (or *zazen*).

This morning we are all gathered at Loubès-Bernac, the original name of the village where the Lower Hamlet is located, including the community of nuns directed by Sister Gina. The monks and nuns of the other two hamlets have come here, mostly in small vans, for this exercise. With concentrated expressions on our faces (most of them relaxed, but some showing effort) and small, slow movements, we walk. Each of us finds our own individual rhythm, one which fits with our inbreath, and our outbreath. These walks always have at least one substantial pause, and this time it is beside a calm little stream. We wait for a timeless moment, calm as the stream itself, and then resume our walk.

What on earth *is* the purpose of this? If I had to answer the silent question behind the stares of those passing farmers, could I somehow communicate to them that we are learning to be totally present in the here and now? Would I find a way to tell them that when we are fully present and aware of walking, savoring every step, then our inner chattering and agitation miraculously subsides, so that we can at last feel and taste the immensity of the present?

Later the same day, Thay's talk returns to this theme:

> *When you walk, you are really walking. You are 100 percent invested in walking, not holding anything in reserve. Every day of your life, you must walk in order to go from one place to another. Why not make every one of these walks a meditation? It is best to walk slowly, but even when it must be quickly, it can be a meditation. Observe the monks and nuns here at Plum Village. When they walk, they really walk. They don't chatter to each other while walking. When you talk to someone, you are not really walking. Or rather, you are walking like a machine, not like a meditator. One thing at a time!*
>
> *When you feel a need to speak to the person you are walking with, just stop. And they will stop too. At that moment, you are 100 percent in what I call*

"speaking meditation." When you have both said what you have to say, then you can resume walking. Everything in its own time. One thing at a time. Walking, or speaking, take your choice. But not both at once.

Try to practice this in your daily life. Even when you go to the bus stop, make it into a walking meditation. Even if your surroundings are full of noise and agitation, you can still walk in rhythm with your breathing. Even in the commotion of a big city, you can walk with peace, happiness, and an inner smile. This is what it means to live fully in every moment of every day of your life. This is something which is possible.

All of us who live here at Plum Village have signed an agreement with the flight of stairs we most often use. We agree to always practice walking meditation on these stairs, whether going up or down. Even on these stairs, we find a rhythm with our walk and our breath. We try to never take them absent-mindedly. When we realize we have climbed several steps in forgetfulness, we go back down and climb them over again. Over twenty years ago, I signed such an agreement with my stairs, and it has brought me great joy.

When I climb a mountain, even when I fly in an airplane, I use this same method. Walking meditation is with me everywhere I go. Why not try it yourself? You are just as capable as I am of signing an agreement with your stairs, and of finding happiness in every step you take. And you will see: even a few weeks after signing this agreement, you will observe a *positive change in your life, and progress in your practice. This is something which is possible.*

This is something which is possible. This seems to be one of Thay's favorite phrases. For his most experienced students, it is a reminder and a constant source of encouragement. It is quite different from many spiritual teachings, which propose long, arduous training and lofty, distant goals which may seem inaccessible at times. In contrast to them, this is a reminder that it is possible for us to make immediate contact, here and now, with our truest and noblest nature. And we do it by being fully aware of what we are doing. Just breathing, sitting and walking. If we lapse into forgetfulness—as we surely will at times—we simply return to this awareness, with no indulgence in self-judgment or guilt.

We need not search for any magical cornerstone of enlightenment. The precious building-stones of the temple of our awakening are already before us, disguised as the most ordinary acts of everyday life. It is through them that we make progress in the realization of consciousness.

This of course includes eating. At Plum Village, silence reigns during meals. People's gestures at and around the table seem almost ceremonial. Before the meal, everyone stands in line holding their plate, bowl, and utensils. The line passes before tables containing large dishes of food: rice or other grains, bread, vegetables, occasionally eggs or cheese, and often a dessert. Simple, healthy, well-cooked, vegetarian food. Sometimes people have to wait a long time during large retreats. But no one shows impatience—on the contrary, the expressions on their faces are relaxed and unperturbed. After all, an unexpectedly long wait is an excellent opportunity to practice.

We advance slowly. When we have served ourselves, we choose a table which still has a few vacant places. We place our food upon the table, and bow to it briefly, with hands together in gesture of prayer. This little bow is no mere formality, but a silent form of "saying grace": an expression of gratitude for this food, which, like the pippala leaf, contains all the riches of the cosmos. This simple gesture evokes the endless time and effort it took for this meal to appear, going all the way from the cooks in the kitchen back to the plowing of the earth, the planting of seeds, the sunshine, rain, and harvests.... And it is also an acknowledgment of the sacrifice of one form of life for another: our own. Indeed, this brief, eloquent bow reminds us that the entire universe is contained in this plate before us.

After taking our seat, we must wait a little longer. The custom here is to wait until everyone has been served before eating (except for those occasions when there are too many visitors for this to be practical). The custom is also to eat slowly, one bite at a time, chewing your food well and savoring the taste of it. This is certainly good for digestion and reducing stress, but it is even better as a lesson in Zen: when you eat, you simply eat. One thing at a time.

Generally, the only words exchanged during meals are those which are strictly necessary. But this, too, has its limits, and the human need to talk has been acknowledged in the custom of a special gong which rings toward the end of the meal. This is the signal for people to speak a bit with their neighbors, if they wish—but softly, and never in a chatty way.

Another custom is for everyone to wash their own dishes afterward. This means more waiting in line at the basins set out on tables for washing and rinsing. Yet when one gets used to it, even this becomes an unhurried, enjoyable meditation. It is true that newcomers often find these slow, silent meals difficult at first. But they soon discover that this way of eating offers far more joy than their usual way, so mechanical, and full of distraction and agitation.

The same thing applies to "work meditation." For at Plum Village, everyone works. On the wall of the dining hall is a large board which assigns tasks for the day to each person: washing pots and cleaning the kitchen, housework, gardening, and other indoor and outdoor tasks. There is never any lack of work to be done, yet the word "work" takes on a different meaning here. It is more important *how* the work is done than *how much* is accomplished. Like eating and walking, work is an opportunity to practice full consciousness. At Plum Village, work is never a mere obligation, something which has to be done in order to "make a living." People work without hurry or agitation, and mostly in silence. Our first day of work here was not so easy, because of our deeply-ingrained habits and attitudes. This pace and way of working went against our reverence for efficiency, our assumption that the more time you can save, the better. But what are we saving time for? More work? Having fun? Surely the deepest joy in life comes from living in full consciousness. If this is so, then we must stop sacrificing consciousness in order to "save time." Our whole relationship to time must change, if we are serious about meditative awareness as a priority, a higher value than those of efficiency and material results. In Thay's teaching, there is no doubt of the central place of meditative awareness:

> *Meditation is something that you can practice at any time in your daily life. At any moment, you can invoke full consciousness, and see things in depth. You can follow your breath while watering the plants, for example. You can really look at the plants, and perhaps even speak to them. This is true meditation. It can also happen*

*as you drive your car. This will bring you peace, and
you will be a better driver.*

*And what is peace? It is the absence of conflict and
violence within us, and the presence of harmony and
well-being. Peace is to be cultivated. Its seeds have
always been there, in our minds and bodies. But these
seeds need to be recognized. We need to be in touch
with them constantly, for this helps them to manifest
and flower.*

The longer the retreat lasts, and the more deeply we experience this teaching, the more we are able to see the extent of
the hidden violence in our lives. We are amazed to see that
our lives have in fact been based on violence. Of course it
does not seem to be violence, for it is very cleverly hidden.
But we see it now, especially in "small" things, the little ways
we tyrannize our body by forcing it, shoving it around as if it
were a machine, feeding it in ways which are not good for it.
But now we see this without guilt, and begin to treat our old
friend, the body, with the kindness and respect it needs and
deserves.

*You have neglected your body. You have caused it
to suffer by the way you eat, the way you drink, or
perhaps smoke ... or simply by the loveless and mechanical way you treat it. Yes, you have inflicted suffering
upon your body, and now the time has come for
reconciliation. This can begin right now, simply, with
conscious breathing. Breathing in, I am aware of my
body. Breathing out, I smile at my body.*

This is not some new-age invention by a popular Buddhist
guru, as some might suppose. It is a 2,500-year-old teaching

which comes directly from Shakyamuni Buddha. Thich Nhat Hanh has been extremely skillful in selecting and adapting Buddhist scriptures to modern needs. Those who are more familiar with his adaptations than with the original sources may be surprised at this passage from the Sutra on Full Consciousness:

On your first breath, you breathe a long breath, saying: "Breathing a long breath in, I know I am breathing a long breath in. Breathing a long breath out, I know I am breathing a long breath out."

On your second breath, you breathe a short breath, and say: "Breathing a short breath in, I know I am breathing a short breath in. Breathing a short breath out, I know I am breathing a short breath out."

Repeating these two breaths will enable you to get rid of distractions and useless thoughts. At the same time, it will bring you into touch with the present moment. Distraction is the absence of full consciousness. *Breathing in full consciousness returns you to your true life.*

Then follows a list of fourteen other breathing exercises with many purposes, some of which are to generate calm, joy, happiness, awareness of bad mental habits, concentration, awareness of impermanence, and letting go. This long series ends with the statement: "Once you have mastered letting go and liberation, you can live in joy and in peace. Nothing more can prevent you from it."

Conscious breathing can also be used like a healing laser beam. It can be directed at will to different parts of the body. For example, the eyes:

Breathing in, I am aware of my eyes. Breathing out, I smile at my eyes.

This is a very powerful exercise. We so often take our eyes for granted, forgetting what marvels they are. This is an opportunity to express wonder and gratitude for the many services they perform, for the joy and pleasure they give us. We may even ask our eyes to forgive us for any suffering we have unconsciously inflicted upon them, perhaps by over-working them, or using them in poor conditions.

This method can be used to send compassionate awareness to any part of our body—even the brain:

> *You have overworked your brain. You have forced it to be active day and night, even in periods of rest: thoughts, memories, fantasies, concepts, emotions, sensations.... You do not know how to give your brain a chance to really rest. You continue to think and reflect, yet these reflections are often useless. Even when your thoughts bring depression, anger, and despair, you keep on thinking, and thinking.... Sound sleep eludes you, for even in your dreams, you continue to suffer. You go to the doctor for pills, but these give only temporary relief at best, and may become just another way of abusing your brain.... The fact is, you must learn how to rest. You must learn to be kind to your brain.*

Be kind to your body—this is a phrase which keeps recurring at Plum Village. Meditation on the breath also helps us to uncover the myriad little ways we have of being unkind, even merciless, with ourselves. Not only do we force our body to perform as if it were a machine, we actually lose awareness of it, which is probably the worst habit of all. No wonder it sometimes rebels or breaks under the strain by falling ill! When this happens, we are finally forced to be aware of our body. Yet we should be just as aware of it when it is functioning perfectly. The body thrives on this simple awareness, attention, and gratitude.

However, it would be a mistake to see this teaching as essentially a set of breathing techniques, or techniques for health and well-being. The techniques, however useful, are secondary. The essence of the teaching is breathing *consciously*. This simple act of awareness is the door to freedom. This is an open secret, so simple that it is hard for many people to accept. We become aware of our breathing. And when our mind strays (as it will), we simply notice it, and bring our attention back to the breath ... as often, and as many times as appropriate ... and without any hint of judgment or self-aggression.

Thay is at his most eloquent and enthusiastic when he speaks of conscious breathing. Here, we arrive at the heart of his teaching:

> When we practice conscious breathing, our attention is totally devoted to the breath. Everything else is set aside. As we breathe in, our attention is on breathing in. As we breathe out, our attention is on breathing out. This is deeper than thought can reach. Breathing in, I know I am breathing in. Breathing out, I know I am breathing out. It is possible for us to rejoice in every inbreath, and rejoice in every outbreath. The simple act of breathing is marvelous. It is a miracle. It is the fundamental act of life in this body. You are alive! So breathe, and be aware that you are alive.

> Breathing in, I know I am alive. Breathing out, I smile at my life. This will bring you much joy and happiness.

Every minute that is given to us is also a gift to the entire universe. No need to think or reflect, for you are literally in your inspiration, and joy can arise naturally. Breathing in, I know that my inbreath is calmer; breathing out, I know that my outbreath is calmer. With the practice of full consciousness, not only does the quality of your breathing improve, it penetrates your entire body and mind.

What teaching could be simpler? And yet ... the problem is, because we have been breathing ever since we were born, we think we know all about it. We take it for granted. We have long developed the habit of breathing unconsciously. And yet this ability in itself is a miracle. As soon as we learn to breathe consciously, we can see how amazing it is that this act is both voluntary and involuntary. Breathing in and out, we know we are breathing in and out, and we are filled with a calm and joy which passes understanding. Here is where the path of the spirit opens before us.

This is not some idea or belief, it is based on solid experience. During the Vietnam War, Sister Chan Khong lived some very difficult years, with many appalling experiences. In her book *Learning True Love*, she talks about how she reacted to bad news—and there was much bad news in those days. At first, she reacted like most people: tensing up at first, thinking over and over about it, and then feeling overcome by despair. However, one day she decided to stop racking her brains, thinking over and over about how to deal with some bad news she had just heard. Instead, she started walking. She took short steps, and watched her breathing. And experienced calm. Soon, she grew skilled in this technique. When the news was very bad, it would take her longer. But sooner or later, deep calm would return to her. With this practice, she also learned that whenever decisions had to be made, they arose from a much deeper source, and came more easily and naturally.

It is not hard to find reasons why this is supposedly impractical for someone who leads a busy, modern, professional life. But this is merely rationalizing our bad habits. If this practice could work for Sister Chan Khong amidst the severe and demanding conditions of the war, it can work for us. No matter how busy we are, we can always find time to become aware of our breathing.

Thich Nhat Hanh frequently reminds us that our bodies and our minds have great need of repose. Very few people in today's hyperactive contemporary world respect this need. Even when they have ample amounts of leisure, they continue to live stressfully, restless and agitated even in their amusements, reacting violently to adversity, and allowing themselves to be constantly invaded by negative emotions such as fear, anger, worry, and anxiety. This has become almost the norm, and conditions would seem to doom things to become still worse. But this grim fatality can be broken. The first crack in the prison wall appears with the simple act of *allowing ourselves repose*. This might require that we work less, but its meaning is much deeper than that—as we have seen, we can even find repose in the midst of work. This is why conscious breathing, as practiced at Plum Village, is also a method of healing.

When we feel unwell for any reason, we tend to rush to our medicine cabinet or pharmacy, and if that doesn't solve it, see a doctor. If the condition persists, we often indulge in worst-case scenarios, which of course only increases our stress. Such reactions show we have lost touch with the knowledge that our body has a profound intelligence of its own, with access to tremendous powers of healing. The main obstacle to this healing is our own mental agitation, and the beliefs which result from it. We rarely give ourselves a chance to heal naturally.

The more we practice breathing in full consciousness, the more we see that this reaction of rushing to stuff ourselves with pills whenever symptoms occur is actually a form of violence. Such violence can prevent natural, deep healing. Of course there are times when we need the help of doctors and medicines, but a life lived in full consciousness will almost always result in a vast reduction of the need for such interventions.

Whenever we find ourselves with five or ten minutes to spare, Thay recommends that instead of reaching automatically for a magazine or some other form of distraction, we use those minutes to practice conscious breathing, or perhaps some other method of deep relaxation that works for us. Even if you are working in an office, this conscious "time out" can only improve your efficiency. However, Thay also reminds us that we must "resist the current" which dominates modern life, so as to protect ourselves from fatigue.

Even when we take a vacation, we must resist this current speed. In most Western countries, workers are given a month or three weeks (in the worst cases, only two weeks) out of the year for "vacation," a word which originally means "emptiness." Yet they rush off to "have fun," multiplying activities, trying to avoid boredom at all costs, and often returning to work in worse state than before. Like our work, our vacation time is immeasurably enhanced by using the opportunity to practice meditative breathing, sitting, and walking.

If you are new to this practice, simply allow your attention to come to the breath, and remain there, without attempting to change its rhythm or alter it in any way. If it is shallow, let it be shallow. If it is deep, let it be deep. Just stay with the breath, as if listening to the rhythm of the tides. This will bring you calm and deep refreshment.

9 ～ *Looking Deeply*

*M*editation is of course the foundation of life at Plum Village. We have already described this, but we have yet to give a more complete account of Thich Nhat Hanh's original approach to this ancient practice. As we noted previously, virtually anything can serve as the focus, or content, of a meditation exercise: a rose, a cloud, a leaf, a stone ... the content is not essential, nor is it essential whether the meditation is a long one or a short one. What is essential is what Thay calls *looking deeply*.

What does this mean? Consider the rose, for example. We easily see, and enjoy, its freshness, its color, and its smell. But if we stop here, we have only touched the surface. When we *look deeply* at the rose, we see that it was not so long ago that this beautiful flower was only a small bud. And it will not be that long until it wilts and dies. As Thay says:

> *When a flower wilts and falls upon the ground, it contains the knowledge of its own renewal. It knows it will decompose into the soil from which it came, awaiting a new manifestation. The flower returns to its source, only to bloom anew when the time has come. Thus the bud opening on the stem is not so much a birth as a manifestation of form. And its*

wilting is not so much a death as an end to this form, making way for a new one.

The same principle is at work in all living beings, whether trees or humans. This is the meaning of the sign which hangs on the walls of the three monasteries at Plum Village: *You are not a creation, you are a manifestation.*

Looking deeply means seeing this truth, within and beyond the outer form. It changes the way we see everything, including our personal destiny. When I look deeply into my "self," I see that my existence was already implicit in my ancestors, and that I will exist in my descendants. This is why I was never born, and will never die. When conditions were right for me to manifest in this form, I manifested in this form. That is all. And inasmuch as I live this truth, I am beyond any fear of death.

One of Thay's many ways of illustrating the meaning of *looking deeply* is through his meditation on a piece of paper. When speaking of this before the assembly at Plum Village, he begins by actually holding up a blank piece of paper:

> *If you look at this paper as a poet does, you might see a cloud floating in it. After all, it was made from the wood of trees, and trees must have rain in order to grow, and rain comes from clouds. So the cloud is an integral and indispensable part of this paper's existence. This is why we say that the paper and the cloud inter-exist. You won't find that word in a dictionary, but its meaning is clear from the prefix and the verb.*
>
> *Still looking deeply at this paper, we find the sun. Without the sun, no forests for paper—in fact, no plants at all. So we can see that the sun is also here. It and the paper inter-exist. But we do not stop here, we continue*

to look deeply—for where are the limits of this looking? We catch a glimpse of the woodsman who cut down the tree and brought it to the paper mill.... And suddenly we may see fields of wheat as well. After all, the woodcutter needed his daily bread, and it had to come from grains of wheat. And now we notice that his father and mother are there too, present in this same piece of paper. All of this was necessary in order for this paper to exist.

Now, if we look even more deeply into this piece of paper, we find ourselves. Why? Simply because we are necessary in order for the paper to be perceived as such. Your mind is in this paper, as is mine. In fact, we now begin to see that everything is in this piece of paper. How could we ever find anything that is not in it? Forests, rivers, the earth, the sun, the stars, all of time and space are here. Everything inter-exists with this paper. Truly, our dictionaries need this new word, for to exist is to inter-exist. Being is inter-being.

If we try to remove any of these elements, there can be no paper. The sunshine, the clouds, the woodcutter's mother, the stars, or your own mind: if we take any of these things back to their source, there is no more paper. So we see that this paper is completely composed of "non-paper" elements. Thin as it is, this piece of paper contains the entire universe.

All the universe in a sheet of paper? An odd image, perhaps, but no more so than the meditation on the pippala leaf. The more time one spends with Thay, the more one realizes that, as with the Buddha, his entire teaching can be seen as a series of variations upon this theme of looking deeply. On one occasion, he picked up a box of matches, opened it, took out a match, and held it up before the assembly.

> *The flame is not visible now. But if I look deeply at this match, I can see it shining. The flame is not yet here, but all the conditions for its manifestation are. I have only to strike the match—or rather, to invite the flame to appear ...* (striking the match into flame).... *If you are an experienced meditator, you don't have to wait for this manifestation in order to recognize the presence of the flame in the match.*

On another occasion, he speaks of a farmer sowing sunflower seeds in his field. It will be months before the plants grow and mature. But a farmer who is used to looking deeply can already see a field full of magnificent sunflowers as he goes about his sowing. In the same way, an organic gardener might see huge heads of lettuce while spreading out the compost.

10 ∾ The Illusion of Death

$\mathcal{W}$hen we look deeply into the problem of death, we catch a glimpse of the fundamental mistake we are always making. It is the same mistake we make when we are unable to see the flame in the match. When someone dies, our deeply-ingrained habit is to see them as having totally disappeared, merged into nothingness and oblivion—just like the flame when it is blown out.

Thay illustrates this by taking a match in one hand, and a piece of paper in the other. Waving the paper before us, he says, "Now let us see if this match really has the power to annihilate this piece of paper." Striking the match, he sets the paper afire, holding it deftly, allowing it to burn entirely before placing the ashes in a tray. Then he invites us to consider exactly what has happened. Clearly, the paper has undergone several transformations. It became fire, heat, smoke, and ashes. We have all witnessed this, and Thay, at least, felt the heat as he held the burning paper between his fingers. We could not feel the heat, but we saw the light, and if we had sophisticated enough scientific instruments, we could have measured it. This energy penetrated us, and beyond us—far beyond us. How far? There are no limits. Even this tiny act of burning a piece of paper has an effect on the entire universe. From our point of view, it may be negligible, but from a microcosmic point of view, it could be enormous, even cataclysmic.

So we see what a crude error it is to say that the piece of paper simply "disappeared." Its smoke went up to the sky, perhaps joining with a cloud which will someday give rain. Its ashes will be thrown in the compost bin, perhaps becoming beautiful flowers someday. And its light and heat have vibrated out towards incalculable infinity. And these are only the most tangible material aspects, the tip of the iceberg of this paper's transformation and inter-being.

In this way, we can begin to see the error of our stubborn, habitual way of looking at death. What we call "death" is in fact transformation. A dramatic transformation, perhaps, but in no way "annihilation." Being can never be reduced to non-being. As Thay says with a grin, after completing his little demonstration, "To be or not to be—that is not the question."

Barely has the laughter subsided when he launches into a more serious vein:

> Suppose you have lost a loved one. You think they have simply ceased to exist. You are blind to the fact that they are undergoing dramatic changes of form, that they are already involved in a new manifestation. Things are happening very quickly—except in you. You are stuck, imprisoned in one fixed image of this beloved manifestation. Now is the time to practice looking deeply. Now is the time to realize that nothing is lost and nothing is created; therefore, nothing can ever be born, and nothing can ever die. The scientist Lavoisier said exactly this. So you see, you don't have to be a Buddhist in order to see reality as it is. Get rid of your concepts of life and death, and you will find freedom waiting for you. Freedom from the pain

that comes from your concepts of loss, death, and
non-being.

A profound silence fills the hall. Looking around, we perceive tension on a number of faces. Perhaps these people have experienced the grief of losing a loved one? And who among us has not? Perhaps Thay's words are not so consoling after all. Certainly not at first glance. It is hardly consoling for most of us to be told that our beloved has not really died, but has become scattered among the flowers, the clouds, and the stars. Indeed, this could make us feel even worse. Are Buddhists so contemptuous of incarnation as to take comfort in such a thought? It may even seem nihilistic.

But looking deeply into this reveals something quite different. In his journal, *Fragrant Palm Leaves*, Thich Nhat Hanh writes of a night in New York City when he had just walked outdoors after attending a Buddhist meeting. Walking down Riverside Drive, he suddenly noticed the full moon, "appearing like magic in a silver sky, framed by skyscrapers." It was an October evening, and he recalled that his mother had died six years ago during a full moon in October.

> *This midnight moon is as sweet and wondrous as a mother's love. For four years after her death, I felt like an orphan. Then she came to me one night in a dream. From that time on, I ceased to feel her death as a loss. I realized that she had never died, and that my sorrow was founded on sheer illusion. One night in April, when I was still living in the high plateaus of Vietnam, she came to me in a dream. She appeared as she always had, and we spoke in an entirely natural way, without the slightest trace of grief. I had often*

*dreamed of her before, but the dream of her on this
night had an impact like none of the others.*

*I awoke about an hour after midnight, and my sor-
row was gone. I saw that my idea that I had lost my
mother was nothing more than that: an idea. And I
realized that if I could see my mother in a dream,
then I could see her everywhere. As I walked in the
garden drenched in moonlight, I felt this moonlight
as my mother's presence. In truth, I could see my
mother everywhere and anytime.*

These heartfelt words can help us to look more deeply into
the appearance of our loved one being dispersed in the flowers
and stars. The only reason this image horrifies us is because we
are still attached to the illusion that our beloved was *ever* identified with a particular form *in the first place*. They were never
born, so how could they die? It is our attachment to a single,
narrow manifestation that keeps us in loss and sorrow. Life is
not limited to our little earthly existence, and our beloved cannot be limited to one brief physical manifestation. Who they
truly are was not born when this body was born. And even this
body was already implicit in its ancestors' bodies: half of the
genes from the mother, half from the father, and so on all the
way back to time and life immemorial. The point is, none of
this has any existence in itself, separate from the rest. In a sense,
neither we nor our beloved has ever existed, we have *inter-
existed*—we always have, and always will. Only our deep-rooted
belief in separate being prevents us from seeing beyond the
appearance of birth and death, keeping us in sorrow.

This is the true and ancient teaching of Buddhism, as
transmitted by Thich Nhat Hanh. It is radically different
from certain unfortunately nihilistic interpretations.

Which brings us to a central and often misunderstood Buddhist term: *Nirvana*. This can also lead to a shallow or nihilistic interpretation if we do not look deeply. Nirvana is not some sort of blissful blankness into which one is plunged by attaining enlightenment. Nor does it have anything to do with our concept of "nothingness." In fact, Nirvana is the absence of any concept. It is beyond all concepts, all notions of birth, death, appearance, disappearance, time, and space. It is beyond all pairs of opposites. Nirvana is the peace of *not-knowing*. Yet this not-knowing is the very source of wisdom. All wisdom traditions recognize this in one way or another: that concepts and beliefs are dangerous, for they attempt to capture and fix the truth.

Consider the concept of happiness, for example. We tend to believe that this concept is indispensable—how could we possibly function without it? The idea of others' happiness, as well as our own? But we rarely look deeply enough to see that the concept of happiness *requires* that of unhappiness—in fact, without a contrasting concept of unhappiness, it loses all meaning. Failing to see this, we get caught up in the pendulum-swing of these opposites. We become convinced that getting what we want will make us happy. Then, after we have it, we feel a strange, perplexing sense of something missing. And we move on to a new cycle of desire for something else, ad infinitum. This is something we can easily see in our everyday lives. What is harder to see is that this whole structure is a set-up from the start: desire arising from the concept of happiness is by its very nature insatiable. Of course we can and do experience happiness. But if we are to be faithful to our happiness, we must paradoxically give up our concept of it.

The concept of happiness is even more dangerous at the collective level. Those who think they are working for the happiness of humanity contrive and perpetuate some of the most destructive ideologies. Once you begin to believe you *know* what is necessary for "the happiness of humanity," you have taken the first step on the road to persecuting those who disagree. The worst atrocities have been committed "for the common good." If we wish to live in the freedom of full consciousness, we must rid ourselves of all dependence on this concept of happiness. Those who have learned to look deeply, beyond ideologies, beyond concepts, and beyond all the pairs of opposites, never engage in aggression towards others—or towards themselves.

But few human beings, even Buddhists, are quite ready to look deeply into the illusion of their own death when it draws near. We need help. Among Buddhist practices which can help us to do this, Thay recommends reading and reciting the discourse entitled *Teachings to be Given to the Sick*.

The central figure in this scripture is Anathapindika, a very rich banker who lived in the kingdom of Shravasti. Many dialogues give the impression that the Buddha spent all his time with monks, but in this one he is speaking with a house-holder, who also happens to be one of his closest friends and supporters. Anathapindika had originally met the Buddha while on a business trip in a neighboring kingdom, and this meeting shook him to his foundations. He immediately became a lay disciple, and begged his new teacher to come to his home country to teach. He donated a magnificent park to the sangha as an inducement. It was called the Jeta Park, after the name of the local sovereign from whom he had purchased it.

This park became famous because of the many teachings the Buddha gave there. Most of these were for monks and nuns, but there were also many for the laity. On one occasion he even taught a crowd of 500 businessmen who had been invited there by Anathapindika.

One day this devoted disciple became terminally ill. Learning of this, the Buddha visited him at his bedside. Before leaving his friend, he appointed his closest disciple, the venerable Shariputra, to keep watch over Anathapindika, and offer him spiritual counsel in his last days. Shariputra was accompanied by Ananda, who later became one of the most famous of all the Buddha's disciples to posterity.

The dying man complained to the two monks that his pains were increasing, and went into great detail in describing them. In response, Shariputra asked that they all three join together in contemplation of the Three Jewels: Awakening (Buddha); the path of practice (Dharma); and the community (Sangha).

To us, this might seem like a mere pious formula, offered by a monk who is unable to really help the man with his pain. However, after the three men had meditated long together on the Three Jewels, Anathapindika's face became relaxed and radiant, and his suffering diminished.

Why? Certainly not because the Three Jewels were a magic formula. In fact, this same meditation would probably be useless for most people today, especially non-Buddhists. So why did it work for Anathapindika? Thich Nhat Hanh explains this, and the universal lesson to be drawn from it, as follows:

> Shariputra had deep insight. He knew what great joy Anathapindika had derived from his support of the Buddha, the Dharma, and the Sangha. By directing his attention to the seeds of his own happiness, and away from the seeds of his pain, he helped Anathapindika restore the balance of well-being amidst physical pain.

In you, too, there are seeds of pain. When these start to manifest, you must make it your top priority to water the seeds of happiness. This will restore your balance. Hence it is a very skillful response, not a mere formula. If you find yourself at the bedside of someone who is dying, do as Shariputra did: learn to recognize this person's seeds of pleasure, joy, and happiness, and then water them. Make these seeds your focus of communication with the dying one, so as to neutralize pain. This is something which must be learned.

Later in the scripture, we find a series of meditations which are designed to help the dying man break his habit of identifying himself with the various characteristics of his body. These associations are an obstacle to his freedom, and the method used here is a series of meditative negations. first, the sense organs: "These eyes are not who I am; these ears are not who I am; ... etc. And finally, "This body is not who I am." And the corollary: "This mind is not who I am." Identification with the body and the mind which depends on it must be broken, otherwise the fear of death will arise over and over again.[9]

This is followed by further refinements of disidentification with objects of sense-perception, thoughts, the sense of time and space, etc., listed according to the categories of that culture and that era. What is relevant for us today is that through this process of negation, Anathapindika became purified and free of all identification with his physical incarnation. Lightened of this burden of separate identity, he could see the illusory nature of all phenomena, and he knew that there is no birth and no death. Realizing this, he began to weep. Misunderstanding this, Ananda asked him if something has gone wrong with his meditation. But Anathapindika reassured him:

"I am weeping because I am deeply moved. I am so fortunate to have served the Buddha and this community for many years. And yet I have never heard such a profound, precious, and wondrous teaching as the words which our friend Shariputra has spoken today."

The Venerable Ananda then questioned Anathapindika, the householder:

"But do you not know that the Buddha gives this very teaching regularly to the bhikkus *and* bhikkunis *(monks and nuns)?"*

Anathapindika the householder then replied:

"Reverend Ananda, I beg you to convey this message to the Buddha for me: although many householders cannot hear, appreciate, and practice teachings such as the one I have received today, there are others who can. Please tell the Buddha that I implore him to make this marvelous teaching available to everyone."

Anathapindika was then able to die in the fullness of freedom, joy, and enlightenment, attended by the monks.

Thich Nhat Hanh considers this to be a key scripture in two different respects. first, for his students who are on the Buddhist path, especially monastics, it is a scripture which must be studied deeply, and recited as well. Second, he takes Anathapindika's last request seriously: somehow this teaching must also be made available to non-monastics—and even to non-Buddhists. Its message is one of freeing oneself from the hypnotic trance of identification with the body. But even deeper than this is the teaching of fearlessness. Enlightenment and love are incompatible with fear. Again and again, life places the choice before us: love, or fear?

The crucial event that takes place in this scripture is the full awakening in love and fearlessness of an ordinary householder, not an adept or a monk. When reading Buddhist and similar scriptures, we often get the impression that awakening, enlightenment, Nirvana, full consciousness, or however we refer to this supreme value, is something for adepts, unattainable by "ordinary" people.

The good news is that this is wrong. As Thay constantly reminds us, often with a smile, "This is something which is possible." Not just possible for saints, heroes, and monks, but possible for us. But only if we truly devote ourselves, and persevere in returning to full consciousness, not excluding any moment of life from this practice.

> *Every time you return from distraction into deep awareness of your breath, you are in touch with full consciousness. You are a living Buddha. It only takes one experience of living in full consciousness to see that awakening is possible for you. You, too, can realize your true nature if you take the trouble to practice.*

> *When you find yourself at a loss, simply return to your breath. Breathe in consciously, breathe out consciously. Take refuge in full consciousness. Whenever you feel anger, confusion, fear, agitation, whenever you feel lost, this refuge is always there, waiting for you. Full consciousness is our blessed isle. It is totally reliable. In times of loss, instability, or danger, you can always return to this blessed isle, to your true nature.*

11 ❧ *Emotions and Equanimity*

$\mathcal{W}$e have yet to look deeply into another major inter-ference which makes us forget our blessed isle of refuge, and induces us to live in exile from our own true nature: our emotions. Or rather, being caught up in our emotions, and possessed by them. One of the most beautiful and useful teachings in Buddhism is that of *equanimity*. To be in equa-nimity is to not be identified with our emotions. But this dis-identification is not easy to achieve in a stable way. Even the wisest human beings must begin the path to equanimity with work on themselves.

When it comes to mastery of emotions, life is not easy for anyone. We are all subject to violent emotions, whether pain-ful or pleasurable (or rapidly shifting between the two). We have all inherited whole blocks of suffering to some degree, beginning in our childhood. No matter how fortunate we may be in having wise and loving parents, we have still received seeds of suffering from them. And we have often repressed these seeds (typically because as children we knew no other way of dealing with such negativity), burying them in our unconscious. Many other negative seeds come from religious institutions, which distort even the greatest teachings into a form of self-aggression, imposing confusing and toxic obli-gations on us.

This ancient accumulation of suffering and violence in us is like a time-bomb. If nothing is done, it will sooner or later explode, in the form of outer violence, inner violence, or both. Crime, drug addiction, war, and mental illness are only a few examples of the social effect of these bombs going off. It is imperative that we look deeply into the nature of this bomb in us, and learn to dismantle it.

Many people still turn to psychoanalysis, especially in France. Lying on a couch, they are encouraged by the therapist to talk about whatever comes to mind, in hopes that some repressed memory or feeling will bubble up from deep within the unconscious mind. They are also urged to dwell upon the pain they experienced in their childhood—and to constantly look to the past for explanations.

Thay makes a humorous comparison between this process and Buddhist and other spiritual approaches.

> *Notice that the psychoanalyst does not face the client. He is hidden safely behind the person lying on the couch. It is as if he is afraid a bomb might explode. Perhaps he should bring in some sandbags for real protection.... But all this aside, and even if the analyst does face the client, the latter continues to suffer, and also continues to indulge in constant self-judgment. Both therapist and patient collaborate in a dogged search for the origins of the patient's pain in the past. Of course this digging can sometimes be useful, but it often becomes a long, difficult, and excruciating process.*

> *This is a violent approach, foreign to Buddhism. Our only defense is full consciousness. With it, we explore the depths of the present moment, right here and now.*

When we live intensely in the present, the past also becomes accessible, for it is an aspect of the present. The same applies to the future: it is accessible through the vastness of the present. It is useless to dig in your mind so as to get to the past. Instead of such violence, we use the peaceful and natural means of looking deeply.

You have a very competent analyst within you, and it is none other than full consciousness. In it, you are both the one who talks and the one who listens.

Of course we cannot help but feel turbulent emotions—to try to suppress them would be an even worse form of self-aggression. But we can calm them by taking refuge in full consciousness, even while an emotional storm is raging. Only in this way can we gain a natural control over emotions, so that we are not identified with them, and therefore cannot be possessed by them.

To illustrate the grave danger of allowing oneself to become possessed by emotions, Thay recounts a story which is often told in Vietnam, of a soldier who had to leave his pregnant wife to go to war and returned several years later.

The news of his return reached the village before him, and his wife and three-year-old son ran to greet him joyously when he arrived. It was the first time he had seen his son. Following the custom, he prepared to make an offering upon the altar of his ancestors. He asked his wife to go in search of provisions for this ceremony, and while he was alone with his son, he attempted to persuade the boy to call him "Papa," which he had not yet done. But the boy stubbornly refused. When pressured to do so by his father, he blurted out: "But Sir, you are not my father. My father is a man who used to come see my mother at night. She would talk and laugh with him and me, and every time she lay down on the bed, he would lie down too."

The father was shocked and enraged by this. By the time his wife returned with the offerings, he could not even stand to look at her. She was completely bewildered by his attitude at first, but soon began to feel offended in her turn. Since both of them were proud, neither would speak to the other. Thus they began to suffer.

As the day wore on, the situation only grew worse. A bitter, hellish emotion had descended like a spell upon the household, and the family was possessed by it. They should have talked about it, of course. But they refused, each proudly pretending to have no need of the other. In a few hours, real dialogue between them had become impossible. Love had been completely eclipsed by pride and arrogance. The boy could only cry alone in a corner.

Finally the man was ready to place the offering upon the altar. Tradition required each participant to perform four prostrations on the mat. The husband did his prostrations, but he angrily forbade his wife to participate by performing hers. She was bewildered and humiliated by this, but she had too much pride to ask for an explanation, and walked out.

The man then went to drown his sorrows at the village bar. He got so drunk he didn't come home, and stayed away for three full days, drinking steadily. By the end of the third day, his wife was in such despair that she threw herself in the river, and drowned.

Now the father was alone, and had to take care of his son. One night he lit the lamp in their hut, and the boy cried: "Look, Sir, Papa is here!" And he pointed to the man's own shadow on the wall. "Look, he sits and lies down with you, just like he did with my mother."

It turned out that many months ago, the boy had asked his mother why his father never came to their home, as other children's fathers did. In response, the mother invented a playful story: her shadow on the wall was the boy's father. "See, there he is. Look how he moves whenever I do."

The man was of course crushed by remorse when he heard the boy's full story.

Naturally, this grotesque, appalling tragedy could have been prevented if only they had talked. Everything would have been different if the man had said, "My dear, I am very upset by something our son just told me. I would like an explanation from you." This is a simple case of possession by negative emotions, and relatively easy to see through. What is much harder to see is that we are not as different from these people as we might like to think. When we are identified with our emotions, we are just as blind as this man was.

Nothing is more destructive of human relations than holding onto distorted perceptions of the other. And it is enslavement to our emotions that keeps these distortions going. We are all subject to this state of possession, even if we maintain the cool façade of someone in control of their emotions. Sometimes the worst explosions erupt in "unemotional" types.

But Buddhism also warns against the notion, current in pop-psychology, that by expressing one's emotions (especially anger), one can "ventilate" them and become less controlled by them. This is a dangerous illusion, especially in the case of anger. Indulging in "emotional expression" often gives rise to a vicious circle of negative feedback from others, and leads only to greater possession, not liberation. We have all had the experience of giving in to an impulse to "express" something which we profoundly regret later.

Nor is repression of emotions acceptable, for obvious reasons. So we are faced with a seeming dilemma: if neither expression nor repression works, then what is left? Many people cannot imagine a third alternative, unfortunately. But there is one in Buddhism, and it is the practice of full consciousness. This is an awareness which embraces emotions, especially in their physical, embodied aspect. But it is not driven by them, nor does it need to express them to others.

How are emotions experienced by a person who lives in full consciousness? To give us a more vivid sense of this, Thay uses the analogy of a tree. Consider how the tree behaves in a storm. It moves very dynamically with the winds, but without violence. It simply bends with the movement—it has no need to "express" itself as a tree, no need to "react" to the storm.

> *If you watch its branches being whipped around, you may get the impression that the tree is very fragile. But if you turn your attention to the trunk, and think about the roots sunk deep in the earth, you will have a different impression. You will realize that the tree is strong, and stable in its foundation.*
>
> *In the same way, when you are beset by an emotional storm, don't let your attention remain at the level of the thoughts racing around in your brain. They are like the branches and leaves of the tree. You also have a tree within you, and it has a solid trunk and deep roots. Let your attention descend there, from your head down into your body. It is dangerous to remain at the level of the head. Come down to your trunk, to a spot which is located just a couple of inches below your navel. Let your attention remain there. And practice*

conscious breathing. If you are sitting, you can deepen this breathing. Observe the movement of your belly, and give it 100 percent of your attention. Breathing in, my belly rises. Breathing out, my belly falls. Keep your attention on your breath even as the storm rages in your head. You are safe, just like the tree. This practice must become your refuge. It will protect you from emotional violence. When you do it, you know that an emotion is just an emotion. It is not who you are. It comes, it stays for awhile, and then it subsides. Just like the storm.

This may seem simple, but how difficult it is to practice consistently! Especially when dealing with powerful negative emotions, such as jealousy, anger, and fear. Yet what are our alternatives? If we truly desire to stop falling back into the trance of emotional identification in which most of humanity lives, all the great spiritual and psychological traditions tell us essentially the same thing: we must realize that *we are not our emotions*. But this cannot happen through the mind alone. We must realize it on a "gut level." It is significant that Thay directs our attention precisely to this level in the preceding exercise. Conscious breathing is one of the most effective ways to bring this realization into the whole body, not just the head.

12 ～ The Five Aggregates

From most of the accounts we have given so far, one might well conclude that Thich Nhat Hanh's teaching avoids philosophical discourse. It is true that his is a very practice-oriented approach. Yet Thay does not overlook the importance of philosophy, provided it is linked to spiritual practice. A Buddhist philosophical teaching which offers insight into our unconscious habits of identification is that of the five aggregates, or *skandhas* in Sanskrit. Every human being is composed of these five aggregates. They are: the physical organism (*rupa*); sensation (*vedana*); conception (*sanjna*); motivation (*samskara*); and consciousness (*vijnana*). The first and last of these (body and consciousness) are often considered as the primary constituents of the human individual, while the other three (sensation, conception, and motivation) comprise the dynamic relations, or processes, which link body and consciousness.

Thay has us begin with the first aggregate as it applies directly to us: a contemplation of our own physical body. In this practice, we visualize and feel our body in its entirety, but also in its detail, including every part and every organ we know of. Breathing consciously, we flood our body with an attitude of loving kindness. We acknowledge our tendency to take it for granted, mistreating it, perhaps even despising it. We see how we dominate it mentally, burdening our digestive system and liver with various excesses, our brain with distracted, obsessive thinking, and our heart with worries and negative emotions. We see this without judgment, and allow ourselves to feel gratitude for its wonderful service to us. In other words, we *look deeply* at our physical organism.

Then we move to the second aggregate: our sensations. Some are pleasant, others neutral or unpleasant. Some may even be pleasant and unpleasant at the same time. Thay likens this *skandha* of sensation to a constantly flowing river. Sometimes the current is rapid, other times slow, but it is always in motion. "To meditate is to sit beside the river of our sensations," he says. Not to plunge into them and be swept away, but to sit beside them, fully appreciating them. The same as with our emotions, we see that we are not our sensations. We witness their display, giving them neither more nor less merit than they deserve. We also feel loving kindness and gratitude for them, but we see into their ephemeral, illusory nature. We are not deceived by them, nor do we judge them. They are endlessly changing, showing one spectacle after another, from birth to death. The point of this meditation is to be free of our sensations, even the most pleasurable.

The third aggregate is translated sometimes as conception, other times as perception. The reason for this is that the Sanskrit word *sanjna* includes both meanings. This is significant, for it suggests that our perceptions are not simply "given" to us, but are also shaped, and even constructed, by our concepts and beliefs. Modern Western philosophy and psychology have only recently begun to fully acknowledge this constructive aspect of perception.

This *skandha* is also like an ever-flowing river, beside which we sit in meditation. But it has even more potential for illusion than the aggregate of sensation. We are very often the victims of distorted and illusory perceptions, some of which may be quite beautiful. One of the most famous examples is falling in love. This phenomenon very much involves the aggregate we are discussing. When we do not know how to break the spell of identification with this aggregate of conception/perception, we attribute all of our profound emotion and excitement *to the person we are in love with*. We cannot see the extent to which this "perception" is a construction and a projection of our own. Very rarely does our perception of the person we have fallen in love with give an accurate and comprehensive picture of who they are. And when we discover this discrepancy, as we surely will in time, it will be painful and even traumatic if we are identified with the *skandha* of perception. We may even reproach the other for not living up to our "perception" of them in that moment of enchantment.

But we must not blame our illusory perceptions and conceptions, any more than we blame our emotions. By their very nature, they are subject to error and distortion. The problem is our ignorance of how they work, and our identification with them. This is why philosophical and spiritual traditions since time immemorial have placed such primary emphasis on knowing oneself. Indeed, self-knowledge could be said to be the beginning and end of every spiritual path. But an end which is endless, and a knowledge which is inexhaustible.

The fourth aggregate, *samskara*, is often translated as motivation, but this can be misleading. The Sanskrit meaning is much richer, and is also translated in some contexts as "innate tendencies," or "karmic thought forms." Western languages tend to limit the idea of motivation to its manifestation in physical action, but in Buddhist philosophy it begins with thought forms. These may or may not have an ethical dimension. For example, if a person harbors a hostile or vengeful image of an enemy, this is the thought-form aspect of a *samskara*. It may develop further into fantasies, or scenarios, of harming this person, yet go no further than this. Or it may finally manifest in violent action. In Buddhism, each of these three stages is part of the aggregate of motivation, and each has its own karmic consequences. This has its parallel in the Bible proverb, "As a man thinks in his heart, so is he."

Thay insists on the reality of these thought-forms, comparing them to a table. Just as a table is the outcome of the type of wood and materials used, as well as the skill and style of the carpenter, so our thought forms are the outcome of many experiences, concepts, actions, etc. As with the rose, these inter-exist with other phenomena back into time immemorial, perhaps including previous lifetimes. They comprise our karmic tendencies, and so it is extremely important that we become aware of what they are, and meditate upon them, so as not to be identified with them. This is the meaning behind the Zen proverb, so shocking when we first encounter it: "If you meet the Buddha on the road, kill him." Of course this is not a literal incitement to kill anyone, but it is a deliberately provocative injunction to always radically question your thought-form of the Buddha, no matter how approved by Buddhist tradition, for it can never truly represent the reality. Of course this applies to the aggregates of sensation and conception/perception as well as that of motivations, which begin as thought-forms.

Thay points out that both physical and psychological phenomena have thought-forms, or innate karmic tendencies, at their root. These *samskaras* result in all kinds of phenomena, from anger and despair to compassion and enthusiasm. From ugly dungeons of torture to beautiful temples of peace and wisdom. Buddhist philosophy lists fifty-one categories of *samskaras*. Inasmuch as they are phenomena, they are all subject to the law of impermanence: they have a beginning and an end in time.

This brings us directly to the fifth and most important aggregate: that of consciousness. It is only through consciousness that we become aware of the impermanent, illusory nature of phenomena. It embraces all the other aggregates, including the totality of the seeds which give rise to all thought-forms and motivations. Most significantly (and this contradicts assumptions made by certain schools of Western psychology), consciousness also embraces those seeds which are buried so deeply in us that they have not yet risen to the level of personal awareness.

For example, no matter how serene my present state of mind, it is certain that I contain seeds of other states: fear, anger, pleasure, etc. They are dormant now, but can be awakened by the right conditions. Even one event might be enough to trigger an explosive anger in me, which was a dormant, invisible seed only moments ago. If I am lacking in self-knowledge, I can easily be surprised and overwhelmed by the force of this erupting seed. I may find myself saying or doing things I later regret, when the anger has subsided, and returned to its dormant seed-state.

Consciousness is a kind of storehouse of a vast variety of grains—good, bad, and indifferent ones. They lie dormant in us, waiting for the conditions which cause them to sprout. This sprouting can be slow and gradual, or it can be so rapid as to be explosive, as in the previous example.

We can look at this storehouse as a kind of cellar, where all dormant seeds are kept. When they sprout, the tendrils move up into the other levels of the house of our psyche. If I have never engaged in any kind of work on myself, then I will barely even be aware of the existence of this cellar and the seeds stored there. Someone says or does something which pushes my buttons, and suddenly one of these seeds has sprouted up into my living room, forming a noxious plant which takes up all the space there. People who live in self-ignorance are helpless before such events, and engage in acts of violence of all sorts, towards others and towards themselves. One only has to read the daily newspaper to see the kind of world this produces.

13 ∾ *Cleaning the House, Watering the Plants*

*W*hat are we to do, if we wish our lives to be part of the solution, instead of part of the problem?

The first thing is to recognize the existence of these seeds within us, without any trace of self-judgment. The aggregate of consciousness gives us this power, for it is the all-embracing storehouse of these seeds. We do not have to go through some laborious psychotherapy, recalling childhood traumas, in order to be aware of these grains, here and now. And we do not need to describe them in scientific detail in order to know they are there, and feel their potential energy. Knowing we have these grains within us, we are in a vastly better position than someone who does not know them, or refuses to acknowledge them.

The next thing (or rather, the complementary thing) to do is to recognize the positive seeds which are also in our cellar, and cultivate them. Perhaps the most important of these is compassion. Compassion for ourselves can enable us to look upon the most negative, toxic seeds in our cellar without self-judgment, with calm and loving kindness. These good seeds in us can allow us to see, with equanimity, that we, too, have the seeds of selfishness, cruelty, and murder in us. By abundantly watering and nurturing our good seeds, we neutralize and inhibit the growth of the negative ones in a natural way.

This is a teaching which, in one form or another, is common to all authentic spiritual traditions. Thay clearly favors the term *full consciousness*, but this is not fundamentally different from what certain traditions may refer to as the Holy Spirit, Bodhicitta, Self-realization, Selflessness, Presence, or Enlightenment.

The image of the dark cellar obviously recalls models of the unconscious in Western psychology. However, the latter tends to focus on the negative aspects of the unconscious, and forget the positive ones. Also, as we noted earlier, the Western "unconscious" is more dualistic, and is not embraced by a larger consciousness as it is in Buddhist psychology. This approach only increases the fear with which we regard our negative grains. We know from experience that when they arise to the level of conscious thought, we become anxious or unhappy. This encourages us to do everything we can, often resorting to very clever self-deceptions, to block these negative energies from consciousness. Sometimes we succeed for awhile. But the grains are still there, ready to sprout up again when conditions are right. Even worse, they may poison our lives by growing in the dark, kept there by our repression and lack of simple honesty with ourselves. Then they grow into complex knots which we cannot untangle, and which slowly begin to choke us. The longer this situation goes on, the more we become, as Thay says, "like a bomb ready to explode." Such explosions can do great damage to the psyche, even blowing out the partitions between the cellar and the living room, creating terrible suffering, neurosis, and madness.

Sensing that something must be done to prevent this, we often look in the wrong directions, finding temporary or illusory solutions. A typical escape is to plunge into work and social activities, filling our appointment calendars, multiplying our networks of relations and acquaintances (but rarely achieving deep friendships), filling our time with distractions. Some of these may even involve work for noble causes. Yet when these are undertaken as an escape from full consciousness, they lead sooner or later to an experience of "burn-out." Whether we escape through drugs, through work, or through charitable activities, we are still involved in *distraction*. We use the word here in Pascal's sense: our vain attempts to escape from the simple confrontation and communion with our own soul. A "noble" distraction may buy us more time than an unhealthy one. But sooner or later the day will come when the grains of suffering we have never wanted to face grow into a jungle and overwhelm us. This may result in psychic or physical aggression toward others, or toward ourselves, perhaps resulting in physical illness.

This analogy of the psyche as a house with many rooms, including cellar and living room, is often used by Thay. His talk on this subject was the most intense moment of the entire retreat for French-speakers.

> *Unable to be alone in your house, you are always inviting guests. Your living room is so crowded with them that there is no more ventilation, and the air is saturated with psychic toxins. Just like your blood, your psyche needs good circulation in order to eliminate toxins. You clog it up and pollute it by accumulating dubious guests and useless distractions, so that thought-forms can no longer circulate freely. Furthermore, negative thought forms such as fear, anxiety, despair, envy, and anger are actually growing in your house, becoming quite large. Why are these*

things growing like this? Because of the kind of guests you welcome. For example, when you indulge in unwholesome television, pessimistic literature, and violent movies, you are watering and nourishing the negative seeds in yourself.

Why should it surprise us that our suffering increases, if we continue to water our negative seeds, and neglect our good ones? And all our attempts to prevent the suffering from arising to the level of conscious thought can only worsen it. It is a vicious circle.

But this circle can be broken.

We begin our psychic house-cleaning with a trip to the cellar. Perhaps it has been a long time since we went down there. But our reasons for going down into this cellar (i.e., into an awareness beneath the level of conscious thought) are very different from psychoanalytic delving in the "unconscious," which it may superficially resemble. The main reason is that this cellar is where our best seeds lie buried and neglected. They may be so forgotten that we are astonished to discover how much joy, peace, love, and compassion were lying dormant in the bottom of our hearts. These seeds of joy do not need some lucky event to occur, nor some desire or ambition to be realized, in order to flower. They only need to be watered and nourished with our awareness and attention. If we water them with mindfulness and perseverance, it is never too late for them to germinate and grow again—and when allowed to grow, they will naturally control and reduce the effects of the negative seeds. They will do this without harshness, and with understanding and compassion. It is by neglecting to nurture our positive seeds with attention and recognition that we empower the negative ones to do so much harm.

This is fundamental to Thay's approach. It is has little to do with the strategy of psychoanalysis, which devotes major effort to detecting, analyzing, and re-living these negative thought-forms—with a kind of unquestioned faith that this process of analysis will somehow render them harmless. Thay's approach to psychotherapy is both simpler and more profound:

> I recommend two things: first, you must stop this careless nurturing of things which are not good for you. This means you must stop feeding those unwelcome guests in your living room. Second, you must begin to remove the dams you have built which prevent thought-forms from rising up into consciousness. This is difficult for those who are not practitioners, because they are afraid of this awareness which they have been blocking. But Buddhist practice offers us very effective methods of protection. This problem of how to remove the barriers is naturally and safely resolved by the energy of full consciousness. If you have practiced it during a retreat for even one day, you have already developed your capacity for living in full consciousness. And the same applies even more to two days, three days, or a week-long retreat. And of course you can always practice at home. Do your dishes in full consciousness, walk down the street in full consciousness, drive your car in full consciousness ... and breathe. Every minute you practice will build and strengthen this energy in you.
>
> Then, when you are ready, open all the doors and allow these things to come up as they will. The Buddha was very clear about the need for this. He knew all about the negativity inside us which we are afraid to

face, such as fear and despair. To all the monks and nuns, he recommended the practice: "Breathing in, I am aware of my fear." He told them they must summon and face fear in all its forms. You may remember that there is a chant in our book which mentions this practice for embracing the fear of death: "It is my nature to die. I cannot escape death." This is a basic, primary practice.

This may well explain why many people in the West are turning to Buddhism. We often hear and read of sincere, perplexed, and somewhat worried Christians wondering publicly why it is that people who were born and raised in a country with an ancient Christian tradition are so interested in Buddhism. Surely Christianity has much to offer, with its teaching of the Presence of God, the Holy Spirit, the compassion of Christ. Why are people turning to a foreign religion and deserting their own?

As we have seen, Thich Nhat Hanh never recommends that people desert their own religion. Quite the contrary. But even devout Christians are turning to Buddhism for help, for two good reasons: the decline of meditation practice in the Christian tradition; and the scarcity of psychological insight and skills such as the ones we have been discussing. As Thay says, you can develop your capacity to live in full consciousness by practicing it. You do not need to plunge into books on Christian theology, Buddhist doctrine, or scriptural studies. You only need to learn to breathe consciously and live fully in the most humble, banal, repetitive acts of everyday life. And when you go astray into distraction, simply return, and return again, with no trace of guilt or self-reproach.

The subject of guilt is very much related to the need for psychological insight in Christian practice today. Buddhist psychology cuts through guilt, exposing it as a form of self-aggression. It is also a distortion of an ancient teaching: the original Greek word *hamartia*, which is translated as "sin" in our New Testament, means simply "missing the mark."

All human beings, even those who project the utmost self-assurance, have the same basic fears: fear of failure, fear of aging and illness, fear of death. They try to hide these fears from others and from themselves. They do everything in their power to forget them, hoping they will somehow disappear. Thich Nhat Hanh, on the other hand, teaches us to summon these fears, so that they can be faced with authentic confidence: yes, it is my nature to grow old, and it is my nature to die. I cannot escape this. But if I learn to live my life in full consciousness, being fully present in every moment, then old age and death have no more sting. They, too, are revealed as illusory and impermanent. When I am living totally in the present, I cannot age, because I am ageless. The present moment is the open door to eternity.

Once we truly accept that we will have to die and abandon everything, we are given the power to embrace all other aspects of fear. However, Buddhism also teaches that we are accompanied by the fruits of our actions beyond the passage of physical death, which then become seeds in the next form in which we manifest. This is called *karma* in Sanskrit, and has now become a well-known word in many Western languages. Unfortunately, the word is often misunderstood as a kind of fate, or a system of reward and punishment. In reality, we can transform our karma right now, by cultivating our good seeds. Even though the toxic plants may continue to grow from the cellar all the way up into our living rooms, they will have less and less force. If we persevere in not feeding the noxious plants, and in watering our good ones, they will gradually wither and die.

*You can do this, and you can do it every day. Do not be
afraid. The Buddha is here, and the Holy Spirit is here.
They will sustain you. The Buddha and the Holy Spirit
are none other than full consciousness.*

As we have seen, one of Thay's favorite metaphors is that
of watering plants. Sometimes he says that the main skill he
teaches is selective watering. This skill not only applies to how
we treat ourselves, but how we treat others. It is extremely
important to become aware of this. For example, you may be
watering negative seeds in your spouse, your relative, or your
friend, without consciously realizing what you are doing. But
this unconsciousness in no way absolves you from responsibility. If you are watering the seeds of despair, anger, or fear
in someone you love, then you are creating more suffering
for them. Begin right now to water the positive seeds instead.
This may be done in small, subtle, even apparently trivial
ways. But even the tiny waterings are very important in the
long run, and can be incredibly effective in themselves. As
with Zen practice in general, it is the small everyday things
that are the most solid ground of transformation.

Thay tells the story of a couple from the city of Bordeaux, not
very far away from Plum Village, who came for the celebration
of Gautama Buddha's birth. When he spoke on the subject of
selective watering that day, he noticed that the woman was cry-
ing. Later, as they were leaving, Thay spoke to the man privately,
and told him, "My friend, your flower needs to be watered." On
the trip back to Bordeaux, the man began to subtly practice
selective watering, as Thay had explained to him. This resulted
in such a momentous opening of their souls to each other that
they were both transformed by it. After they arrived home, their
children felt a dramatic difference in her, to the point that it
seemed as if they had a new mother. She had opened like a flower.

This selective watering is something that you must really devote yourself to, and practice every day. If you love someone, make this covenant with them: "My dear, I promise to not water the negative seeds in you, and I promise to water your positive seeds every day. I will do this for your happiness, and for mine." And the other person should do the same for you. This is selective watering. It is not a difficult practice at all, and if you do it consistently, you will very soon experience positive changes, giving you much more breathing space in your relationship.

The very least one can say is that this is worth a try.

The time for change has come, on all levels. We can begin at any time. Why not begin now? There is a story about an Orthodox saint who was asked why more people do not become saints. "Because they never begin," he answered.

We need not dramatize this beginning, for an ordinary act will suffice. The journey of a thousand miles begins with a single step, as the proverb says. It could be a small change in our consumer habits, or simply the practice of more awareness during one of those habits. Whatever we consume, whether it is through our digestive system or through our senses and our mind, the important thing is that it be positive and nourishing. Impressions, too, are food. Awareness of this is just as much a part of the practice of full consciousness as is sitting or walking meditation.

The spiritual adventure is always a movement towards freedom. Freedom from the things which encumber our psychic space, freedom from our resentments, our guilt, and our suffering. This freedom is always and only to be found in the present. "Life is offered to us only in the present," said the Buddha. To which Thich Nhat Hanh adds:

Make your home in the present moment. Then you will see the future become more available, as well as the past. And both can be changed.

14 ∾ *Saved by the Bell*

The first time it happens, we are surprised and bewildered. Even when we know the reason for it, it takes us awhile to get used to this Plum Village tradition. It can happen on any occasion: speaking with someone, working at a task, eating, walking in meditation, or standing in line at mealtime. A bell rings, and everything stops. People stop talking in the middle of a sentence. Everyone stops walking, stops working, stops eating—even those who are in the act of taking a spoonful of rice out of their bowl pause, spoon in midair. Everyone listens, and is still. Then, when the sound of the bell has completely died away, normal activity resumes calmly, as if nothing had happened.

This moment of listening is observed every time any kind of bell rings, outdoors or indoors. If you are within hearing of the clock's bell, you will make this pause every fifteen minutes. Even near a telephone, people stop when it rings. The custom is that whoever is supposed to answer it waits until it rings three times, listening silently along with everyone else. Then they pick it up, and answer. Whatever the nature of the incoming call, this is no mechanical answer.

It may seem like a minor eccentricity, but this practice has a profound effect on us, and on the monks and nuns who live here as well. It is a lesson in vigilance and surrender, a surprisingly effective aid to living in full consciousness, and a pleasure as well. After all, there *is* something special about the sound of a bell.... As Thay says, "The sound of the bell is the voice of the Buddha, calling us home to full consciousness." Perhaps this was the original purpose of bells in Christianity.

Once we are familiar with this practice, the sound of the bell becomes strangely enlivening. It is as if we are called deeper into life by it, back to our true life in the present moment, out of the death of "living in our thoughts." If we are honest with ourselves, we must admit that life without full consciousness is really a kind of living death. No matter how active we are in body or mind, we are not really *here*. We are trapped in the trance of passing time, mechanical time. If this is the only time we know, then when death finds us, we will feel as if we have never really lived. How strange and sad is the condition of those who never see this! They seem outwardly alive, agitated and driven here and there by fear, pleasure, and the whole gamut of emotions and desires. But they are dead inside, especially to themselves.

Thich Nhat Hanh was impressed by the central character in Albert Camus' novel, *The Stranger*. This man, Meursault, had for no good reason killed an Arab man on a beach in Algeria. He was arrested, tried, and sentenced to death; yet this whole process went by like a dream, and he had no real consciousness of what was happening to him. Only a few hours before his execution, he is sitting in his cell, and begins to feel fear. At first he spends much time in vain fantasies of escape, but eventually this comes to a stop. For many days, he has been in a cell with a tiny window from which he can only see a patch of sky. Lying on his cot, whole days pass while he looks at the shifting colors of this patch of sky, changing from day to night. At one point, he notes that he must have fallen asleep, because he wakes up with starlight on his face. He hears noises of the countryside, and night odors of earth and salt arise from below and come into his cell. He feels the wondrous peace of this summer night washing over him like the tide.

What is so interesting about Camus' character is the transformation that takes place in him when he really begins to face his own death for the first time. Even in this callous, fearful, alienated man, the dormant seeds of full consciousness begin to sprout and grow. He no longer cares about the long past or the very short future. He lives intensely in the present moment, his attention on the sky, the odor of the sea not far away, and "the wondrous peace of this summer night."

He finds such unexpected joy and life in the present that when the authorities announce that they are sending a chaplain in to see him, he refuses, saying that he has no need of religious consolation. Nevertheless, an audience with a priest does take place, and he tries to explain that his time is very short, and he cannot afford to waste it talking about God. The priest, possibly offended and challenged by this brazen remark, tries all the harder to drag the prisoner out of the present moment, urging him to think about the future of his soul, etc. But it does not work. All the priest's certainties are worthless to him, because with his new vision, he is able to see through him. He sees a man who is not really alive, not present here and now, but lives only in his head, in his thoughts, fantasies, and dogmas. At least Meursault has three days of real life left to him. This priest is already dead. Thich Nhat Hanh offers this conclusion:

> *The prisoner had only three days to live, and for some unknown reason, he suddenly was able to truly connect with the patch of blue sky. It was the first time he had*

ever seen the sky. Thirty-five years old, and this was the first time he had ever been able to really touch the blue sky. He knew that he had only three days left, and this moment of full consciousness helped him to live totally in the present for the rest of his life.

Sometimes it takes a shock as dramatic as this to make us see the sky for the first time. But gentle means may also be quite effective. After the discussion of Camus' character, Thay told us about a reporter who approached him in San Francisco, eager to secure an interview. Normally Thay does not accept interviews with the press, but for some reason he agreed to a meeting with this man. It took place underneath a giant redwood tree in a park. Thay asked the reporter to have tea with him. The latter was sensitive enough to see that this was not a man who would chat while sipping his tea, so he accepted the tea, and sat down, thinking the interview would take place after tea. Then Thay asked him if he would please forget about doing an interview. Disappointed, but equal to the occasion, the journalist agreed to abandon his quest. In exchange, he received something far more precious than an interview:

I showed him how to drink a cup of tea in full consciousness, savoring this moment of sitting in silent friendship there. And he practiced very well. He deeply enjoyed this moment of having tea together, recognizing his own presence in the world beside the presence of the other. When we finished our tea, I invited him to do a short walking meditation with me. We walked toward his parked car, and on the way, I invited him to look at the sky, and say to himself: "Breathing in, I am aware of the blue sky. Breathing out, I smile at the blue sky." He practiced

*this whole-heartedly. Afterwards, he told me that this
was the first time in his life that he had seen the sky
like this.*

What a lucky reporter! He had come to the meeting with
his head full of questions to ask, questions he probably
thought far more important than drinking tea and looking at
the sky. Instead of answers to these questions, he experienced
a moment of silent communion, walking in full consciousness, and the blue sky as he had never seen it before. Or perhaps
some of his questions about Buddhism *were* answered, and
far more effectively than learned explanations could have
done.

15 ~ Living Permanently with Impermanence

*H*ow are people at Plum Village able to maintain this intensity of living in the present over the long term? Is there not a danger of all these practices becoming institutionalized and mechanical? Perhaps so, but this is not what we, nor other visitors perceive. All visitors we have talked to speak of a kind of shock when they enter the atmosphere of the three hamlets, either for the first time, or after a long absence. This shock is especially powerful for city dwellers. The monks and nuns they meet seem to exude a kind of supernatural calm. There is no hint of agitation in their attitudes or their movements. This is so radically different from what we are used to that we may indeed have an impression of something mechanical or unnatural about it at first, simply because we are so used (and perhaps attached) to agitation in ourselves and in those around us. But with time, a complete reversal takes place: it is this way of life which now seems natural, and the "normal" life outside which seems unnatural. Furthermore, we learn that intensity and relaxation are entirely compatible. We can *relax into the intensity* of being in the present. In this way, we are both more alive, and more relaxed. No wonder people come to consider this as the normal way to be, and the typical urban life as abnormal. In fact, this may require skillful means in dealing with the "re-entry" phase when it is time to return to the city.

When long-term residents walk, every step seems to matter. When they work, they are silent, and their movements are relaxed and graceful. When they speak to each other, they speak in calm tones, never raising their voices. Indeed, it is one's first exposure to this atmosphere that is most difficult. Some people even think about leaving, convinced that this is some kind of utopian illusion, inaccessible ideal, or worse, some kind of cult. Even when they realize the error of this impression, they may still feel that only those with a monastic calling can achieve this way of being.

Sister Gina would challenge this. For her, living fully in the present is a skill than can be developed by anyone. But it is in no sense a mechanical skill. It certainly grows with practice, but it is never finished and perfected. She is the first to admit that she does not live fully in the present 24 hours a day, 7 days a week, 365 days a year. This of course applies to us all. But perhaps the main difference between her and most of us is that she knows how to quickly and simply *return* when her mind wanders off. "When I practice properly, returning becomes easier and easier, and I stay much longer."

Sister Isabelle, who also works as an acupuncturist, suggests that over time, we learn to stop separating the ordinary from the extraordinary. It is this separation which leads to mechanical attitudes about practice.

> Our practice here is not just formal meditation. We especially look for the magic in the most banal, ordinary moments, for there is hidden beauty in every instant of life. Here, there is no real difference between sacred and profane. Nothing is separate from

meditation. This non-dual approach pleases me immensely, for I know now that the goal of my monastic life is to find this Presence everywhere. It is the Presence of Buddha—or, if you prefer, the Presence of God.

This is the same presence of which mystics of all traditions speak with such fervor and ecstasy. But how far will fervor and ecstasy get us over the long haul? Perhaps the core concern hidden in this question is: what happens to this "living in the present" when we are experiencing excruciating physical or emotional pain? Can we really believe these mystics, who assure us that we are saved by this presence, even during the cruelest moments that life has in store for us: serious illness, or the death of a loved one? Surely this is illusory, wishful thinking? Perhaps it is even a bit mad? Can we really be happy in the midst of terrible pain?

Thay's answer is an unequivocal "Yes." He frequently emphasizes this, and cites the Buddha's words, as well as his own and others' experience, in support of his claim that we can be happy in the midst of pain.

The first thing is to stop resisting, escaping, or trying to get rid of the pain. This is not resignation, but skillful surrender. We must learn to tame our pain by totally accepting it, embracing it with loving kindness and attention. We may even speak to our pain, telling it that we are here to offer it love, acceptance, and help. With that typical, indescribable smile of his, Thay says:

> *The next time you feel pain, smile at your pain, and speak to it: "My dear little pain, I recognize you. Yes, I am completely here for you." After this, but only after this, you may practice sitting or walking meditation.*

This is not something we can master overnight. But we definitely grow more and more skilled with practice, and this skill can be cultivated without limits. Incredible as it may seem, we can learn to be happy in any and all circumstances. How is this possible? Strangely, by fully realizing and living the truth of impermanence. As Thich Nhat Hanh writes in *Siddhartha*:

> *The cause of suffering is ignorance—in other words, a mistaken view of reality. The mistake is to attribute permanence to that which is impermanent. Belief in a separate self is the ignorance which is the root of all fear, greed, anger, jealousy, and countless other forms of suffering. To walk the path of freedom means to practice looking deeply, so as to really see the nature of impermanence, the absence of any separate self, and the interdependence of all things. This is the path of the conquest of ignorance. When ignorance is defeated, suffering is transcended. There is no need of any self to attain Liberation.*

There it is again—impermanence. The constantly recurring theme. Like the monk Do-ji in the midst of his dance movements, we paradoxically discover that it is right in the midst of this impermanence, which we have been so afraid to look deeply into, that we find our greatest happiness, and our freedom.

Long live impermanence!

16 ∾ *Sister Chan Khong*

 $\mathcal{A}$ bout a hundred people are stretched out on the floor of the large meditation hall, taking up every bit of the available space. We lie with eyes closed, waiting until the silence permeates everything. Then a voice appears. A low, gentle, feminine voice, so soft that you have to listen carefully to hear it:

"Take your time, and make yourself comfortable. Keep your eyes closed, and relax. And don't have the slightest worry about falling asleep. If you fall asleep, it's quite all right. It only means you have succeeded in relaxing, and that you need it." This soft voice and these words are so effective that one can sense a kind of collective sigh of relief pass over the whole assembly. Indeed, after a few minutes one can detect small, telltale sounds of a few sleepers.

The voice continues, interspersed with pauses. This is an exercise in deep relaxation, a guided meditation which moves our awareness successively through every part and organ of our body. We dwell at leisure on each part, visualizing it, sensing it, giving it our full attention and compassion. And asking it to forgive us if we have ever been harsh or unkind in any way to it. This is also a kind of examination of our conscience with regard to how we treat ourselves. Self-aggression often manifests as forcing the body and brain to work without rest. But it may also consist of forcing the body to "have fun" by ingesting food or substances in excess. This is fun only for the escapist ego. And now is the time to let our body tell us about this, breathing and relaxing in total, non-judgmental acceptance and love, in every one of our organs.

finally all our bodies are completely relaxed after this healing meditation. After a silence, the woman's voice returns, but this time in song. It sings and hums softly, improvising simple, sweet little melodies and phrases. These are so much like lullabies, that many people now succumb to the temptation of sleep.

This is the voice of Sister Chan Khong, a central figure in the Plum Village community. She modestly describes herself as Thay's secretary. But no one who knows her thinks of her as a secretary, for she is one of Thich Nhat Hanh's oldest and closest dharma-companions. She worked at his side in the struggle for peace during the horrors of the Vietnam War, and she continues to work with him to help people all over the world establish peace in their hearts.

If Plum Village had such a thing as a 'Mother Superior," it could only be Sister Chan. People turn to her when they have a special need for a listening ear, an understanding heart, and a mind skilled at finding solutions to all kinds of problems.

Her peaceful, loving, maternal manner belies a life with so many hardships and adventures that it reads like a novel. In her book, *Learning True Love*, she tells how she eventually had to abandon her advanced studies in botany to answer the urgent needs of the suffering people in her native Vietnam. But she was no stranger to this kind of compassion in action—ever since the age of fourteen, she had found a deeper joy and satisfaction in helping and sharing her money with wretchedly poor high-school classmates, than in any effort to attain enlightenment.

Given her early conviction that true Buddhism must be one of social involvement, it seemed inevitable that she would sooner or later encounter Thich Nhat Hanh. Their first meeting took place in 1959, when she was only twenty-one years old. The next year, she wrote him a letter detailing her philosophical reflections on helping the unfortunate: she confessed to him that she rejected the traditional motivation of helping the poor, because of a belief that it will bestow spiritual merit, "racking up points" for some future life, as she put it. She told him that she wanted to help human beings to be happy and free of their suffering now, in the present moment.

Thus began their lifelong friendship. Her first work with him was with the School of Youth for Social Service, which very soon enlisted several thousand volunteers. Far from the Tet offensive, a fierce battle happening around and in Saigon, she worked successfully to prevent opposing sides from fighting, saving thousands of lives. Later, she accompanied Thay on board the ships which sailed to rescue the "boat people" who were in distress.

Shortly before the arrival of the communists, she realized she had to leave her beloved Vietnam.

> At that time I had no more strength, or enthusiasm
> for life. Every time I thought of Vietnam, I wanted to
> die, just go to sleep and never wake up. I felt as if my
> heart were being crushed by a heavy, brutal hand.
> For a month, the only thing I was able to do was to
> follow my breathing, putting my total attention on
> the inbreath and the outbreath, all day long. Every
> time I stopped, I fell into the darkest despair.

From the moment she arrived in France, she felt dazed, as if she had entered into a strange, other world. The sight of all these people coming and going, sitting in cafés, laughing, going to concerts, movies, and plays ... and not being at war. How could these people have any inkling of the horror and misery which she had witnessed and endured? It would take her some time to adjust to being safe from war, yet living in a foreign land where the seeds of war are still present. A new, and more peaceful adventure awaited her.

She helped Thich Nhat Hanh to establish a community next to the forest of Othe, not far southeast of Paris, called "The Sweet Potatoes." The basic idea was a monastic community which welcomed non-Buddhists, as well as visitors, much the same as that of Plum Village. But there was only one small house available and it soon proved to be insufficient for their needs. Since Thay needed a warmer climate with more sunshine, they first looked in Provence, the southwest, and a number of other places. finally, they found a dozen or so acres in Dordogne, a beautiful region of southern France, not far east of Bordeaux. The property, near Thénac, had three run-down buildings.

This was a difficult period for them. Thich Nhat Hanh was famous in Vietnam, and well-known in the US, but not in France. He had only a few of his own books with him, and they were in Vietnamese. But the word spread quickly among Vietnamese expatriates of this extraordinary monk's presence in France. Both recent refugees and those who had lived in France most or all their lives came to see him and offer material support, overjoyed to find a major Buddhist spiritual teacher living in France, and one who spoke their own language.

The need for more space become urgent. For one thing, the local authorities were looking sternly upon the crowded conditions at Thénac. The community decided to purchase a second piece of land a few short miles away, towards the border of neighboring Tarn-et-Garonne. But the local authorities had decided they didn't want these Vietnamese. For complex bureaucratic reasons, a sub-prefect decided to revoke all their permits, effectively putting an end to the community.

This was a heavy blow. But Sister Chan Khong could not resign herself to this defeat, and went into action. She asked for a personal meeting with the sub-prefect, but was refused. She sensed xenophobic discrimination at work, and in order to maintain her peace of mind, she doubled her practice of walking meditation, and touching the Earth.

> *I thought to myself: OK, this man does not want to see me. Very well, every time I think of him, I will send him good energy, the energy of Buddha, the energy of God. So I did this, and my heart was totally at peace. Thinking about it again, I realized that perhaps these people have no idea who we really are. In this country, people talk a lot about cults these days, and this creates fear. Until this moment, I had been over- whelmed by the "injustice" committed against us, and I thought these people must be racists. Then, when I was calmer, I sent this beautiful energy to that man, and felt totally at peace. I saw the fear in him, fear of cults, fear spread by the media.*

> *Then something came to mind which I had forgotten: during the war two famous French political figures, Jacques Chaban-Delmas and Jean-François Poncet, had met with me and expressed friendship and solidarity with our cause. So I sat right down and wrote to them, asking for their help. They readily agreed, and every- thing was soon resolved.*

But as time went on, even these two monasteries at Thénac (the Upper Hamlet, for men) and at Loubès-Bernac (the Lower Hamlet, for women) were not enough for the growing number of visitors, especially during retreats. At the tiny village of Dieulivol, about nine miles away, there was a beautiful piece of property for sale. Like so many areas of France, this entire region was in the throes of depopulation and decay, because of the destruction of small farms and regional economies by pro-agribusiness policies. The local officials had been unable to generate new income through a vacation and recreation center, which had failed. They agreed to sell the land to the Buddhist community, but it was clear there was uneasiness and mistrust in the air.

This was beautifully dispelled by an idea of Sister Chan's. Near the property was an ancient grotto and a lovely 12th-century chapel. For many generations, people had gathered at this chapel once a year for an annual festival. But with rural depopulation, this custom was dying, as was the church itself. Only a handful of elderly ladies turned up on the festival day now. Sister Chan Khong promised the mayor of the area, and other local residents, that she would attend the ceremony. So the mayor and a few other notables said they would also attend this time, along with the circuit priest of the area. They were astonished to see her arrive with the entire monastic community, some 200 monks and nuns. The Christian members of the Plum Village community took communion, and the Buddhists brought bells and candles, as well as a group of children. The latter walked in slow procession, carrying candles, and singing: "Breathing in, breathing out, I am blooming as the flower, I am fresh as the dew. I am solid as the mountain, I am firm as the earth—I am free." Everyone was happy, and deeply impressed, including the priest. For the first time in many years, this ancient festival had come alive, but not in a way anyone could have predicted.

Naturally, this was the beginning of a warm and solid relationship between the community of Plum Village and the surrounding French communities. The annual festival at the old church still continues, now accompanied by an open house day at all three monasteries.

For Sister Chan Khong, engaged Buddhism is not limited to action at the community and social level. It also includes helping with interpersonal relationships. We have already mentioned her counseling of couples in relation to the Beginning Anew practice. She is often sought out, especially by members of the lay community, to help with family counseling. She tells of a sullen, rebellious adolescent boy who was brought by his parents:

> *He sat down with his feet propped up, pointing directly at my face. I could see that he was doing this to offend his parents, and it worked, because they were furious. But I prevented them from scolding him, because I wanted to gain his trust. When the parents had finished stating their point of view, I turned to the boy, and said: "Now it's your turn to say what you don't like about your mother and father. It could be that you don't understand them. They certainly love you, no doubt about that—but maybe you feel that they're trying to force their point of view on you. Or perhaps they just haven't understood what it is you really want."*

> *It turned out that this boy had plenty to say. His parents respected the rules of the game, and allowed*

him to speak as long as he wanted, with no inter-
ruptions. When he was finished, I said: "My desire
is to be as objective as possible. I've been trying to put
myself in your place. Now I want to try to put myself
in your father's place, and then in your mother's place.
In any family, the essential thing is to understand
each other. People must be allowed to express them-
selves freely in order for this to happen." So we went
on talking, and by the end of the meeting everyone
was very happy. The last thing I asked of them was to
do a meditative embrace. In this practice, everyone
hugs each other with awareness of their breathing,
for three full breaths.

This meditative embrace is a very important practice. However, it is not at all a part of Buddhist tradition. Thich Nhat
Hanh admits that the first time a Western disciple asked him
for a hug, he had a reflex of repulsion. In the East, disciples
do not hug their teachers! But later, he reflected on this. He
realized that many Westerners valued this expression, and
were accustomed to it. Since he now lived in the West, perhaps
he should allow this expression. On the other hand, he knew
that hugging could easily become a banal, meaningless gesture.
In order to allow this expression, yet preserve its authentic
spiritual quality, he devised the formula of the meditative
embrace, and asked those who practiced it to take three deep,
conscious breaths together.

Many people have testified to the healing power of this
form of meditation. A number of couples who are students
of Thay's have followed his suggestion to practice it whenever a problem arises between them. This returns them to a
realization of what a source of happiness they are for each
other. And it reminds them of how precious, and impermanent,

it is to be alive and breathing together in each others' arms. This practice is often sufficient to restore a shattered harmony.

One of the most important collaborations between Thay and Sister Chan Khong is their project to help Vietnamese children whose lives have been shattered by the war and its aftermath, especially the many thousands of orphans.

This work had already begun before their arrival in France about thirty years ago. At that time they were very concerned as to how to help these children from so far away, in a country whose language they spoke because of the colonial legacy, but which still seemed strange to them. But they were soon to discover that their compassion for these children would awaken a similar response in this new land. Sister Chan Khong will never forget the day when Pierre Marchand, a youth of only eighteen, came to see her with a rose in his hand. This sensitive young man had been deeply moved by a lecture he had attended, where Thay had spoken eloquently of the catastrophic suffering caused by the war in Vietnam. With all the enthusiasm and naiveté of youth, he wanted to organize a big pop music concert, inviting some famous stars, so as to collect a large sum of money for these victims. He had already begun arrangements to rent a large hall in Paris, the Maubert Mutualité, which could accommodate 2,000 people. However, the rent was expensive: 3,700 francs for one evening.

She was reticent at first. This was a large sum in those days, and she had reason to worry about the risk. It seemed like a foolish gamble, especially when she considered that only 25 of those francs could be used instead to feed a child for a month. However, she sensed the seriousness and selfless commitment of Pierre Marchand, and she decided to throw herself into this project, so as to make it a success. At worst, they would barely pay the rent—but even this would at least generate publicity for the cause. She filled her tiny Citroen two-cylinder car with posters for the concert, and drove around Paris putting them up wherever she could, often having to return to places where they had been torn down or covered with others.

The success of the concert surpassed all expectations. The hall was filled to overflowing, and they ran out of tickets. This generated a good sum of money for the cause, but even more importantly, it resulted in a great public awareness of the suffering created by this war. A new committee was created to help hungry Vietnamese children, which still exists today, under the name of "*Partage*" (Sharing). Later, when Plum Village was founded, the profits from the harvest of the 2,000 plum trees went mostly to help these children.

As we got to know Sister Chan Khong better, we had occasion to wonder how she maintains her phenomenal energy, which is more appropriate to someone half her age. We have described only a few of her activities here. There are many others, and she is constantly on call to help with them. One day we made so bold as to ask her. At first she would only joke about it, saying that she had a special battery that ran on atomic energy. It was only later that we learned that her true source of energy was as strange in its own way as the atomic battery of her joke: it is the energy of the planet Earth itself.

As mentioned earlier, her way of dealing with the disappointment of the bureaucratic official threatening to revoke the community's permits was to resort to the practice of *touching the Earth*. As she tells us later, "Touching the Earth is very important for me. With her help, we can heal our body and our soul."

This is a practice which includes prostration upon the ground. It is certainly an homage to Mother Earth, but it is also an homage to our ancestors over the centuries, who have become part of her. These ancestors have transmitted to us their physical matter, their energy, their strength, their virtues— and their mistakes. They are the very weaving of our body, our soul, and our spirit. They are our link to the past, and also to the vast energies of the universe. This is an ancient practice of acknowledgment, similar to those of American Indians and many Asiatic and other peoples.

> When I wake up in the morning, I touch the Earth, knowing that my ancestors are alive in me. When I stand and touch the Earth, I sense my genetic family of mother, father, and grandparents. I see them as young men and women. I do not see my ninety-two-year-old mother, I see a young woman of eighteen, with black hair, shining eyes, and smooth skin. I feel my father as a very dynamic young man.

> Then I touch the Earth again, and offer it all the weaknesses of my mother and father. And I also give it my beloved Vietnam, with all its coconut palms, banana trees, and farmers killed by bombs.

> Then, when I have touched the Earth, I say: "I am the energy of all my spiritual ancestors"—that wonderful, humble monk I met once; all those Buddhist practitioners in the small provincial town I came from; all my friends in Saigon, the men and women who did such beautiful work there; and my friends in the sangha here, all the Vietnamese, French, Americans, Germans, Dutch.... From all of these beings, I am receiving such a fantastic energy. I can send this energy to that little girl inside me, that child

who had so many wounds, and because of these wounds was sometimes stubborn and violent.

Since Sister Chan Khong has now lived so much of her life in France, she has discovered new roots, and new spiritual ancestors:

My spiritual Earth-ancestors in France are the people who tore down the Bastille, and overturned feudal laws. Of course Robespierre went too far, and killed many people, but there is no doubt that great progress happened as a result of the French Revolution. Society became more humane, and I am a beneficiary of this compassion. Now I touch the Earth and receive the energy of my new ancestors. I loved the book Les Misérables, *and I can feel the character Gavroche in myself, as well as Marius and all those beings who had such a desire to do good. I touch the Earth, and the whole world is in me. I feel rich and strong. From my very first days in France, I rejoiced in the peace and freedom of this country. What a pleasure it was to be able to travel around without having to ask for a permit, as I had to do for even a short distance in Vietnam. These things must not be taken for granted. Our ancestors struggled for them.*

17 ∿ *The Five Precepts*

*T*he retreat has come to an end, and people are preparing to leave. We look around at others' faces, and look within ourselves, remembering our impressions at the beginning. There is no doubt that the faces we see are far more relaxed, and that people are completely at ease with each other. All the feelings of shyness or withdrawal which some of us felt on the first day are gone. There is unanimity in our happiness at having shared a week (only a week?) of such intensity together.

However, on the very last evening some people expressed a subtle feeling of something like apprehension. It was not that they were unhappy or worried about anything—far from it. On the contrary, they felt filled with the blessings which a week of living in full consciousness had brought them. They wanted this state of grace to be an enduring way of life for them, yet they foresaw that when they returned home, they would be confronted with the same old atmospheres and difficulties of daily life, atmospheres which they had been escaping for this last week. They would be returning to a life of paperwork, taxes, money problems, tensions at the workplace, tensions in the family, bad news on television and other media, and for those who live in big cities, traffic jams, pollution, crime, and violence.

It is the perennial re-entry problem. What can be done to help us through it? Certainly we can make resolutions. And we can make changes, such as creating a meditation space in a corner of our house or apartment. Some of us will follow Thay's suggestion and sign a contract with our stairs. Others will join a local sangha group, if there is one, or practice walking meditation in their yard, if they have one. But whatever solutions we find, all of us sooner or later discover the fragility of these resolutions made at the end of a retreat. How can we overcome this?

One of Thay's principal guides for remaining vigilant in everyday life is the *five Precepts of Full Consciousness*. These apply to every instant of life. They can be practiced in a spontaneous manner. And, for those who desire to make a serious, formal commitment, a ceremony is arranged, in which they vow to follow these precepts for the rest of their life.

At first glance, these precepts may resemble other sorts of pious or moralistic vows, but Thay insists that they not be taken as absolute rules which we must follow, and feel guilty if we fail to do so. The essential nature of the precepts is a kind of beacon which we should always be guided by, knowing that it is impossible to actually attain it finally and for all time. The only strict injunction for those who take the vow (and here there is no room for laxity), is to take the time to recite the precepts at least once a week. And they must be recited slowly, savoring the meaning of all the words. Even here, a partial vow is possible: if there are certain precepts which one feels not yet ready to follow, one may recite only the others.

Here are the *five Precepts of Full Consciousness*, also known as the *five Steps of Training in Full Consciousness*, and the *five Wonderful Precepts*:

Prologue

The five Precepts are the foundation of a happy life. They offer the skills for protection of life, for a life which is beautiful and worth living. They also offer a potential way to enlightenment and freedom. Listen to each precept and say "Yes" silently, every time you see that you have made an effort to study it, to practice it, and to observe it.

First Precept

Aware of the suffering caused by the destruction of life, I vow to cultivate compassion and learn ways to protect the lives of people, animals, plants, and minerals. I am determined not to kill, not to let others kill, and not to condone any act of killing in the world, in my thinking, and in my way of life.

Second Precept

Aware of the suffering caused by exploitation, social injustice, stealing, and oppression, I vow to cultivate loving kindness and learn ways to work for the well-being of people, animals, plants, and minerals. I vow to practice generosity by sharing my time, energy, and material resources with those who are in real need. I am determined not to steal and not to possess anything that should belong to others. I will respect the property of others, but I will prevent others from profiting from human suffering or the suffering of other species on Earth.

Third Precept

Aware of the suffering caused by sexual misconduct, I vow to cultivate responsibility and learn ways to protect the safety and integrity of individuals, couples, families, and society. I am determined not to engage in sexual relations without love and a long-term commitment. To preserve the happiness of myself and others, I am determined to respect my commitments and the commitments of others. I will do everything in my power to protect children from sexual abuse and to prevent couples and families from being broken by sexual misconduct.

Fourth Precept

Aware of the suffering caused by unmindful speech and the inability to listen to others, I vow to cultivate loving speech and deep listening in order to bring joy and happiness to others and relieve others of their suffering. Knowing that words can create happiness or suffering, I vow to learn to speak truthfully, with words that inspire self-confidence, joy, and hope. I am determined not to spread news that I am uncertain of or criticize or condemn things of which I am not sure. I will refrain from uttering words that can cause division or discord, or that can cause the family or the community to break. I will make all efforts to reconcile and resolve all conflicts, however small.

Fifth Precept

Aware of the suffering caused by unmindful consumption, I vow to cultivate good health, both physical and mental, for myself, my family, and my society by practicing mindful eating, drinking, and consuming. I vow to ingest only items that preserve peace, well-being, and joy in my body, in my consciousness, and in the collective body and consciousness of my family and society. I am determined not to use alcohol or any other intoxicant or to ingest foods or other items that contain toxins, such as certain TV programs, magazines, books, films, and conversations. I am aware that to damage my body or my consciousness with these poisons is to betray my ancestors, my parents, my society, and future generations. I will work to transform violence, fear, anger, and confusion in myself and in society by practicing a diet for myself and for society. I understand that a proper diet is crucial for self-transformation and for the transformation of society.

It is only natural to feel apprehension about committing oneself to such a path. Who could possibly feel capable of keeping all these resolutions? Some might even feel that these precepts represent a harsh, outmoded moralism which has no relevance today. But all of these reactions miss the true meaning of the precepts, for they are not intended as absolute rules, nor as dualistic statements of good and evil. Above all, they must never be used as inducements to guilt-feelings, which are so destructive to a true spiritual life.

Here is Thay's answer to a question which someone asked at the end of the retreat:

No one can live the five Precepts perfectly—not even the Buddha. For example, when I eat, I kill. Even when I drink water, I kill the micro-organisms in it. Do you really believe your bowl of cooked vegetables is totally vegetarian? A scientist can prove to you that many micro-organisms were killed during the cooking. But the point is not to try to be a perfect vegetarian. The essential thing is to eat in such a way that full consciousness is possible, and to maintain and cultivate compassion in yourself. That is all. Someone who lacks compassion is incapable of establishing a true relation with other creatures. They isolate themselves. Therefore, to cultivate compassion and understanding is to be able to truly communicate with others. Happiness becomes possible for you when you can communicate, and be at one with others.

So if the fruit is not ripe, I advise you not to take the vow of the five Precepts. You must not force yourself—that would be a form of violence. You cannot receive the five Precepts until you can look deeply.

You cannot take on everything at once. If you don't have a compass, and you need to go north, you can follow the North Star. But that doesn't mean you will be able to reach the North Star. It means you will be able to go north. There is no need for you to be perfect. As I have told you, even the Buddha is not perfect in the five Precepts of Full Consciousness. The Buddha must also walk, and when he walks, he crushes invisible creatures beneath his feet. Avoid too much rigidity in the way you see things. You must enter into the essence, not into the form.

For me, the five Steps of Training in Full Consciousness are a practice of freedom.

One can go still further in this practice of precepts. Some people with long experience in practicing the five Precepts, and who have done many retreats at Plum Village, request to enter the Order of Interbeing. In this, they vow to follow fourteen additional precepts, and they also submit themselves to greater demands regarding compassion, detachment, and transformation. Members of the Order of Interbeing can be identified at Plum Village by a special kind of brown-colored garment.

A key distinction of members of this order is their vow to open themselves to the universal, and to abandon all narrow beliefs and points of view. The first few precepts of the Order are well worth quoting:

> *Aware of the suffering caused by fanaticism and intolerance, we vow not to be idolatrous about, nor bound to any doctrine, theology, or ideology, even Buddhism.*

> *The Buddhist teachings, like all systems of thought, are guiding means, not absolute truth. They help us to practice looking deeply, and to develop our understanding and compassion. They are not doctrines for which we will fight, kill, or sacrifice ourselves.*

> *We must not think that the knowledge we presently possess is changeless, absolute truth. We will avoid being narrow-minded and bound to present views. We will learn and practice non-attachment from views in order to be open to receive others' viewpoints. Truth is found in life and not merely in conceptual knowledge. We will be ready to learn throughout our entire life, and to observe reality in ourselves and in the world at all times.*

> We will not force others, including our own children, by any means whatsoever, to adopt our views, whether by authority, threat, money, propaganda, or even education. However, through compassionate dialogue, we will help others renounce fanaticism and narrowness.

Perhaps it was this spirit of understanding, tolerance, and respect for other faiths and beliefs that attracted us to Plum Village in the first place. It is the main reason why people of all races and creeds feel at ease there. And surely we are all being invited to practice these precepts of interbeing, if not to join the formal order of that name.

A man once told Thay that he could not take vows of refuge, because he enjoyed drinking wine. The answer was the following:

> I ask you to look more deeply, beyond the surface of things. No vow of refuge can make you a true Buddhist in any case. The habit does not make the monk. It could be that you are already a true Buddhist who has not taken refuge. If you are devoted to living in full consciousness, if you know how to taste an orange in full consciousness, you are already a Buddhist. You don't have to become one. There are non-Buddhists who are more Buddhist than Buddhists. We must beware of words and appearances. Are you certain you are not a Buddhist? No. One cannot be sure of being a true Buddhist or not. Look deeply, and realize that there is no separation.

> If you can enjoy every step as you walk in full consciousness, if every step brings you peace, assurance, and joy, then you are a practitioner. It matters little

whether you are called a Buddhist. This is not what
is important.

We conclude this portrait of a teacher and his community by a quotation from the Buddha himself, from a text of which Thich Nhat Hanh is fond, because it summarizes both the Buddha's teaching, and his own.

The setting is a festival day in the magnificent park of Nigrodha, where the Buddha and his monks had been invited by King Suddhodava. The most eminent figures of the kingdom were present, along with thousands of people eager to see and hear this young monk about whom everyone was talking. After a meal eaten in silence, the king asked Gautama for a teaching. The Buddha answered with a discourse whose conclusion has reverberated down through the millennia, as if directed to all of us today in this world so full of suffering and violence:

> *Suffering is only one face of life. If we can see its other, marvelous face, we will have happiness, peace, and joy. When our hearts are free, we can touch the wonders of existence. When we have fully understood the truth of impermanence, of the emptiness of self, and of the interdependent arising of all things, we realize how magnificent this life is—our own bodies, our states of mind, the branches of purple bamboo, the golden chrysanthemums, the limpid running water, and the brilliant moon.*

> *Because we are trapped in our suffering, we lose the capacity to enjoy the miracles of life. When we tear aside the veil of ignorance with deep understanding, we discover the vast realm of peace, freedom, and nirvana, which is the extinction of the illusions born*

of ignorance. This is the end of greed and anger and the beginning of peace, joy, and freedom.

Honorable guests, take the time to contemplate a stream of limpid, running water, or a ray of autumn sunshine. Are you able to experience peace, joy, and freedom? If you are always trapped in the prison of sorrow and anguish, you are forever blind to the marvels of the universe, which include your breath, your heart, your body, and your mind. The way I have discovered enables you to transcend sorrow, anguish, and all other afflictions, by looking deeply into their true nature. I have shown this way to many others—and they have also been able to discover and verify it for themselves.

∾ *Notes*

1. Sanskrit *shunyata*; often mistranslated, and misinterpreted, as an absolute "Nothingness" or "Void."

2. *Tathagata* (Sanskrit) literally means "the one who has come." It is traditionally applied to the Buddha.

3. Nirvana (Sanskrit) literally means "blown out." Many Buddhist teachers, including Thich Nhat Hanh, interpret this as meaning "emptied out" of any clinging to separate selfhood.

4. Actually the French *baccalauréat*, which is equivalent to two years of college in America.

5. *Sangha* (Sanskrit) means the local Buddhist community.

6. *Dharma* (Sanskrit) in this context means both "teaching" and "way."

7. Père Foucauld was a French explorer and soldier turned priest of the early 20th century who manifested great respect and knowledge of indigenous North African cultures. He was also an influential Christian teacher, regarded by many as a saint.

8. A vow not to enter nirvana, or final enlightenment, until all beings are enlightened and have overcome suffering.

9. In Buddhist terminology, the mind (not the spirit) is considered as an organ of perception along with the other senses.

Books by His Holiness the Dalai Lama and Other Buddhist Titles

Beyond Dogma: Dialogues and Discourses
By His Holiness the Dalai Lama
$14.95 trade paper, 244 pp.
ISBN: 1-55643-218-6

Beyond Dogma presents a record of a 1993 visit to France by His Holiness the Dalai Lama, recipient of the 1989 Nobel Peace Prize. During a series of public lectures and question-and-answer sessions with political activists, religious leaders, students, scientists, Buddhist practitioners, and interfaith organizations, His Holiness responds to a wide range of topics, including: the practice of Buddhism in the West; nonviolence, human rights, and the Tibetan crisis; ecumenical approaches to spirituality; the meeting of Buddhism and science; and more.

Essential Teachings
By His Holiness the Dalai Lama
Introduction by Andrew Harvey
$14.95 trade paper, 152 pp.
ISBN: 1-55643-192-9

"This book is Buddhism purified to its simplest human essence, an essence that transcends all barriers, all colors and creeds. It is a philosophy of the most urgent, practical, active altruism constructed not in a study but lived out at the center of a storm of violence."
—from the Introduction by Andrew Harvey, author of *The Return of the Mother* and *The Way of Passion: A Celebration of Rumi*

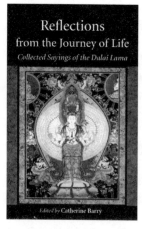

Reflections from the Journey of Life: The Collected Sayings of the Dalai Lama
Edited by Catherine Barry
Translated by Joseph Rowe
$14.95 trade paper, 200 pp.
ISBN: 1-55643-388-3

The Dalai Lama's words of wisdom are collected here from personal conversations with the author, Catherine Barry, a prominent television personality in France. The topics range from violence, death, ethics, and the environment to desire, happiness, religion, and humility. The book is divided into eight chapters and offers contemplations and advice from the highest spiritual authority in Tibetan Buddhism.

Tenzin Gyatso: The Early Life of the Dalai Lama
By Claude Levenson
Translated by Joseph Rowe
$14.95 trade paper, 200 pp.
ISBN: 1-55643-383-2

Tenzin Gyatso focuses on the formative years of the fourteenth Dalai Lama, before he became a worldwide presence and peace activist. It is the authoritative biography of the first twenty-four years of his life as told by a close personal friend and prolific journalist, Claude B. Levenson. This biography follows the long and arduous path that the Dalai Lama traveled from his birth in 1935 to his exile to India at the age of twenty-four.

**Blossoms of the Dharma:
Living as a Buddhist Nun**
By Thubten Chodron
Foreword by Sylvia Boorstein
$16.95 trade paper, 242 pp.
b&w photos
ISBN: 1-55643-325-5

This book gathers some of the presentations and teachings from a 1996 conference in Dharamsala, India, on "Life as a Western Buddhist Nun." His Holiness the Dalai Lama supported the effort of Buddhist nuns to clarify their purpose in taking vows, widening their context, broadening community beyond their own abbeys, and achieving greater equality with men in liturgical matters, especially ordination.

**Buddhist Women on the Edge:
Contemporary Perspectives from the
Western Frontier**
Edited by Marianne Dresser
$16.95 trade paper, 338 pp.
ISBN: 1-55643-203-8

Explore this landmark anthology that covers a wide range of issues around gender, race, class, and sexuality in Buddhism. Contributors include Anne Klein, bell hooks, Miranda Shaw, Tsultrim Allione, Shosan Victoria Austin, and others. These essays range across issues of lineage and authority; monastic, lay, and community practice; the teacher-student relationship; psychological perspectives; and the role of emotions.